Long Vowels &
Double Letter Sounds

Wing Wing Phonics 3

Published by Nexus Co., Ltd.
5 Jimok-ro, Paju-si, Gyeonggi-do, 10880, Korea
www.nexusEDU.kr

Author: Nexus Contents Development Team
Publisher: Sangjin Lim
ISBN: 978-89-93164-05-3 68740
978-89-93164-06-0 (set)

Printed in Korea ⑧

Long Vowels &
Double Letter Sounds

Nexus Contents Development Team

NEXUS Edu

Contents

ZOO

Unit 1 Long Vowel Aa

Emma invites Willy to her house. She is baking a cake for him.

-a-e

cake	lake	bake	wake	cape
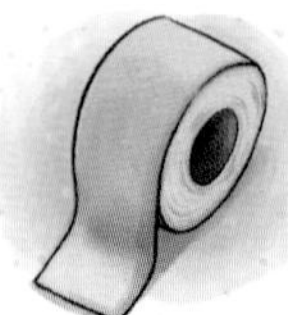				
tape	lace	race	cane	vase

Listen, Repeat and Write  track 01

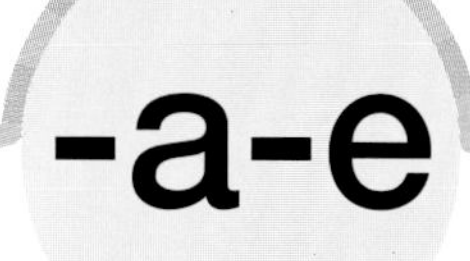

-a-e

wake

bake

vase

lace

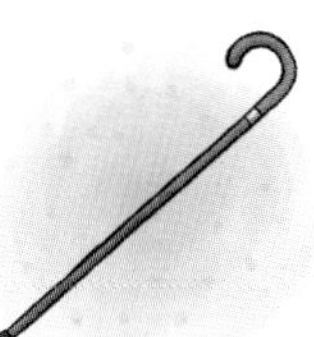

cake

lake

race

cane

cape

tape

Listen and Circle 

1.

2.

Listen, Check and Match

1. 
Ⓐ Ⓑ

2. 
Ⓐ Ⓑ

3. 
Ⓐ Ⓑ

4. 
Ⓐ Ⓑ

Listen and Fill in the blanks

1. Emma likes to  ______________ a  ______________.

e, k, b, a　　a, c, e, k

2. Look at the girl in a  ______________ with red 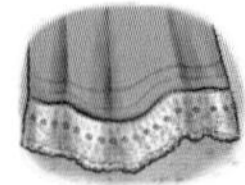 ______________.

e, p, c, a　　l, e, c, a

3. My grandmother drops a 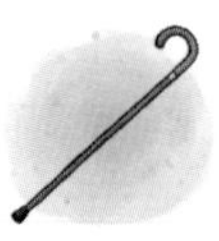 ______________ in the  ______________.

e, c, a, n　　k, a, l, e

Listen, Read and Play

Today is Rabbit's birthday. Koko bakes a cake for Rabbit.

Koko goes to the lake. Rabbit is under the peach tree by the lake.

Koko: Happy Birthday, Rabbit! Here's a birthday cake for you!

Rabbit: Oh thanks, but I don't eat cakes.

Koko: Oh...then, what do you want?

Rabbit: Hmmm.... Your cape is pretty. I like the red lace.

It will look nice on my table under my flower vase.

Koko: Oh.... Uh...okay, you can have my cape with red lace.

Write the words with long /a/ sound in the story.

Unit 2 Long Vowel Ee

Emma's family has a picnic on the beach.

-ee-
-ea-

bee

tree

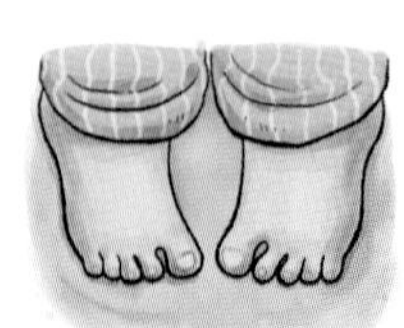
feet

teeth

sea

tea

beach

peach

meat

seat

Listen, Repeat and Write

peach

beach

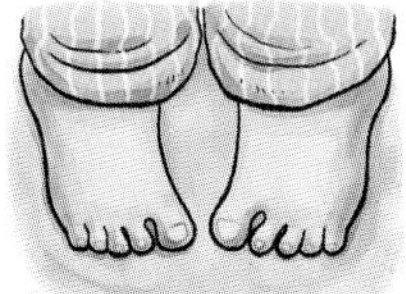

feet

tea

tree

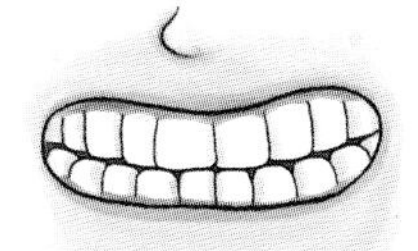

teeth

sea

bee

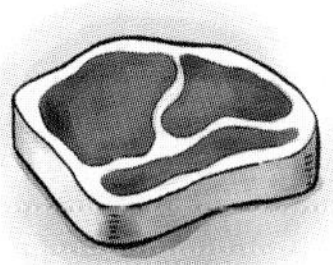

meat

seat

Listen and Circle

1.

2.

Listen, Check and Match

1. tree Ⓐ Ⓑ
2. sea Ⓐ Ⓑ
3. beach Ⓐ Ⓑ
4. seat Ⓐ Ⓑ

Listen and Fill in the blanks

1. There is a  ____________ on a  ____________.
   e, b, e a, h, c, e, p
   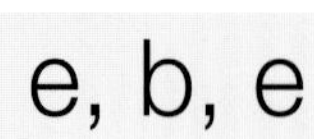

2. Emma has  ____________ and  ____________ in the mornings.
   e, t, a, m a, e, t
   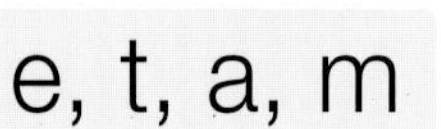

3. A panda has 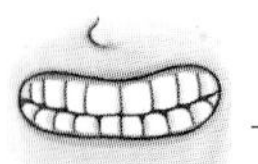 ____________ and two 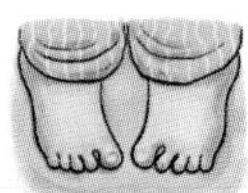 ____________.
   e, h, t, e, t t, e, e, f

Listen, Read and Play

It is a beautiful sunny day at the beach.

Koko and Bobo find two seats under a tree.

They sit and drink juice.

Bobo: Wow, there are many people in the sea!

Koko: Bobo, do you want to go swim in the sea?

Bobo: Nah...I ate a big lunch.

Koko: What did you eat?

Bobo: I had a peach, some meat and a bee with honey.

Koko: You ate a bee?!!

Bobo: Uh...It just flew into my mouth!

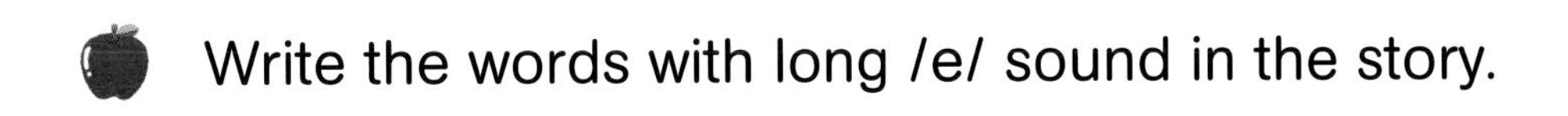

Write the words with long /e/ sound in the story.

Unit 3 Long Vowel Ii

It is Emma's wonderful May calendar.

-i-e

bike	hike	bite	kite	fire
			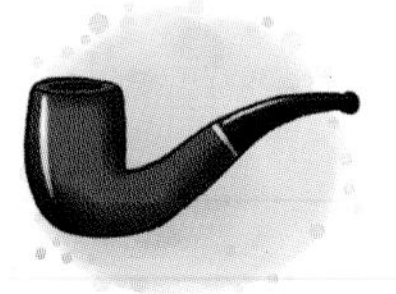	
tire	dive	five	pipe	wipe

Listen, Repeat and Write

 track 03

-i-e

five

dive

bite

tire

wipe

pipe

kite

fire

hike

bike

Listen and Circle

1.

2.

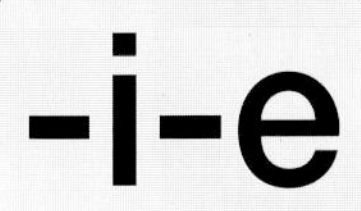

Listen, Check and Match

1. 

Ⓐ Ⓑ

2. 

Ⓐ Ⓑ

3. 

Ⓐ Ⓑ

4. 

Ⓐ Ⓑ

Listen and Fill in the blanks

1. The man with a  ____________ goes on a  ____________.

i, p, e, p　　　e, i, k, h

2. A  ____________ is on  ____________.

r, e, t, i　　　i, r, f, e

3. Willy is flying  ____________  ____________s.

e, v, f, i　　　i, k, e, t

Listen, Read and Play

Tomorrow is Children's Day!

Koko: Let's have some fun tomorrow!

Bobo: Let's ride our bikes.

Koko: Sure, and let's go on a hike!

Bobo: It will be hot, so we can dive into a lake!

Koko: Yes! We can dive five times!

Bobo: And we can fly a kite!

Koko: Yes! Then, you can help me clean my dad's pipe!

Bobo: Uh....that doesn't sound fun...

Write the words with long /i/ sound in the story.

____

____

____

1 Listen and write the letter.  track 04

l k

b

f v

b k

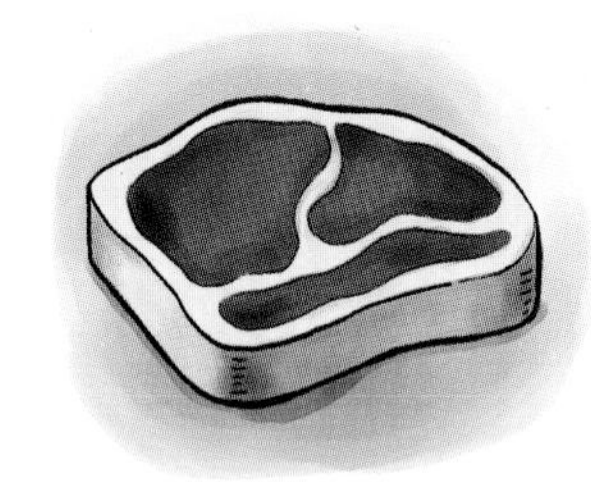

m t

h k

 Listen and circle the correct word. 

race
rece
rice

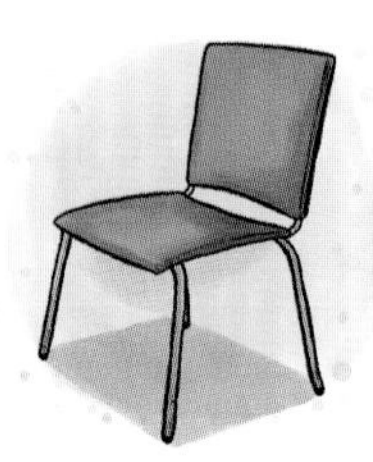

seat
seet
seit

bake
beke
bike

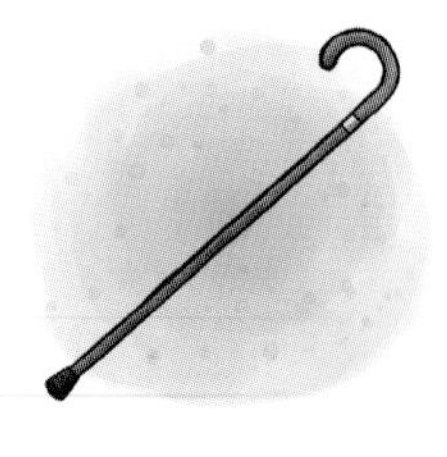

cane
cene
cine

peach
peech
peich

kate
kete
kite

3 Connect and write.

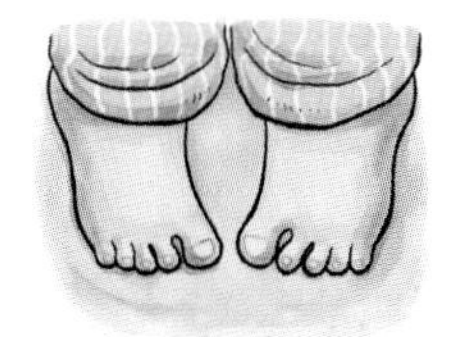	f	eet	______
	t	ite	______
	w	ake	______
	b	ape	______
	f	eeth	______
	t	ipe	______
	w	ire	______
	b	each	______

4 Listen and fill in the blanks. 

1. Koko: Happy Birthday, Rabbit! Here's a birthday c____k____ for you!

   Rabbit: Oh thanks, but I don't eat c____k____s.

   Koko: Oh…then, what do you want?

   Rabbit: Hmmm…. Your c____p____ is pretty. I like the red l____c____.

   It will look nice on my table under my flower v____s____.

2. Bobo: Wow, there are many people in the s____ ____!

   Koko: Bobo, do you want to go swim in the s____ ____?

   Bobo: Nah…I ate a big lunch.

   Koko: What did you eat?

   Bobo: I had a p____ ____ch, some m____ ____t and a b____ ____ with honey.

3. Koko: Let's have some fun tomorrow!

   Bobo: Let's ride our b____k____s.

   Koko: Sure, and let's go on a h____k____!

   Bobo: It will be hot, so we can d____v____ into a lake!

   Koko: Yes! We can d____v____ f____v____ times!

   Bobo: And we can fly a k____t____!

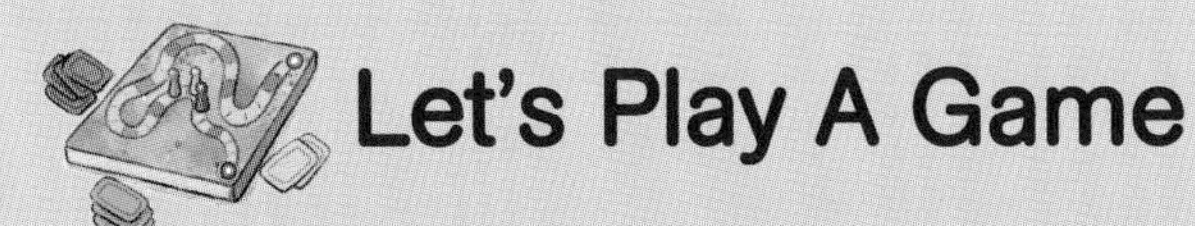

Let's Play A Game

Play a game with your partner. Use a dice and picture cards(A set).

How to Play:

1. Turn all the picture cards upside down and pile them up.
2. Take turns throwing a dice.
3. Draw a card from the deck and read the card.
4. If you can read the card, you score the number that your dice indicates.
   If you can't read, you do not score any.
5. The winner is the one who gets the highest score.

Unit 4 Long Vowel Oo

Emma's friend, Popo, wants a toy house for his birthday.

-o-e

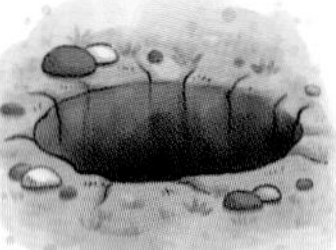
hole

mole

hope

rope

nose

rose

dome

home

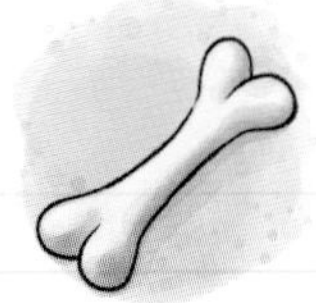
bone

cone

Listen, Repeat and Write

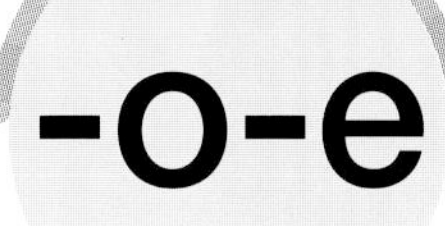

rope

hope

rose

cone

hole

mole

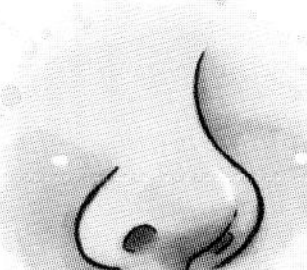

nose

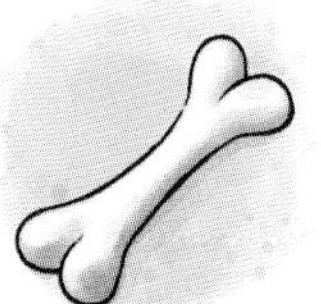

bone

home

dome

Listen and Circle

1.

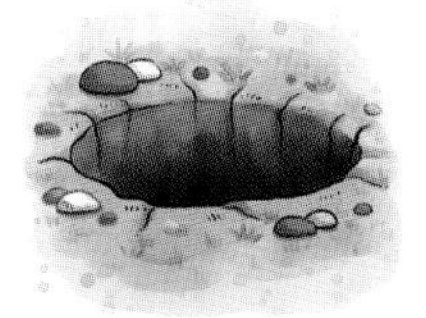

2.

Listen, Check and Match 

1. 

Ⓐ Ⓑ

2. 

Ⓐ Ⓑ

3. 

Ⓐ Ⓑ

4. 

Ⓐ Ⓑ

Listen and Fill in the blanks 

1. The  ____________ digs five 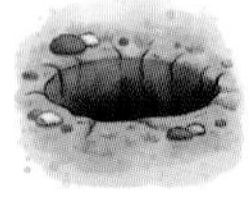 ____________s.
   l, o, e, m   e, h, l, o

2. A dog with a 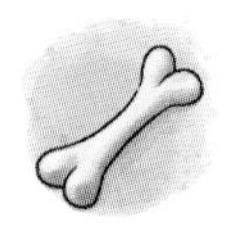 ____________ plays with a 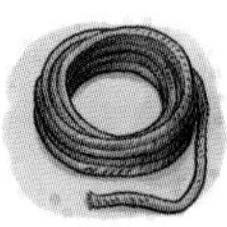 ____________.
   o, n, e, b   e, r, o, p

3. Emma brings a  ____________  ____________.
   r, e, s, o   m, o, h, e

Listen, Read and Play

Koko and Bobo find a hole in the rose garden.

Bobo: Look! There is a hole.

Koko: Oh no! Let's cover the hole with dirt!

Bobo: Oh wait. Look! I see a nose!

Koko: It's a mole!

Bobo: The hole is a mole's home!

Koko: I want to live in a hole, too!

Bobo: Really? I will dig a big hole for you!

Write the words with long /o/ sound in the story.

Unit 5 Long Vowel Uu

Willy and his father are in the living room. They are busy.

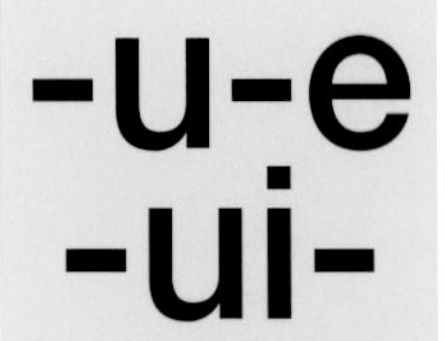

cube

tube

dune

June

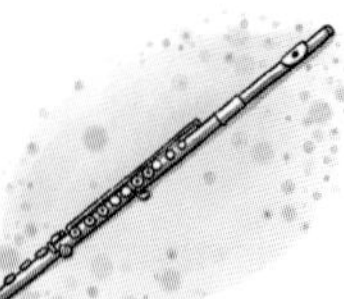
flute

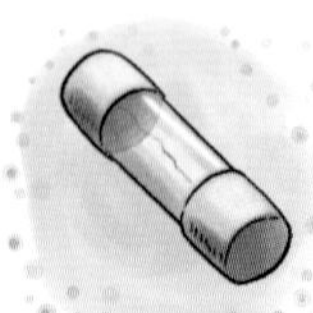
fuse

mule

juice

fruit

suit

Listen, Repeat and Write  track 06

-u-e
-ui-

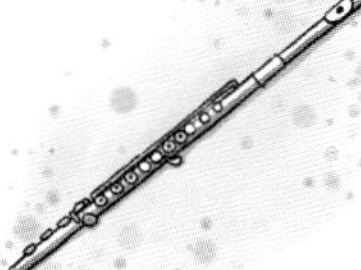

flute

June

cube

dune

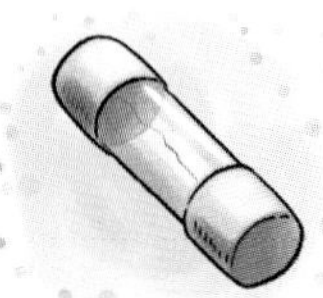

fuse

mule

suit

tube

juice

fruit

Listen and Circle 

1.

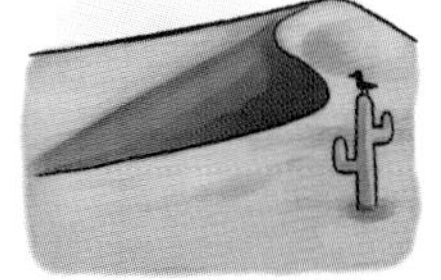

2.

Listen, Check and Match 

1. 

Ⓐ Ⓑ

2. 

Ⓐ Ⓑ

3. 

Ⓐ Ⓑ

4. 

Ⓐ Ⓑ

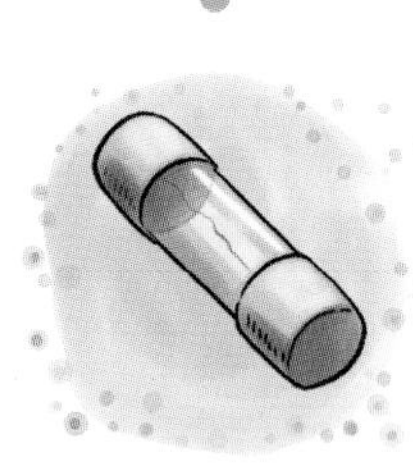

Listen and Fill in the blanks 

1. Mom buys a  ____________ and  ____________ for Willy's school picnic.

b, u, t, e　　r, i, t, u, f

2. Emma got a 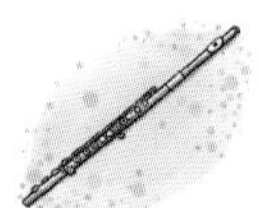 ____________ for her birthday in 

____________.

t, u, f, e, l　　u, e, J, n

3. Look at the  ____________ on the sand  ____________.

l, u, m, e　　n, d, e, u

Listen, Read and Play

Koko has a dream about a mule.

The mule is on a dune. It is a very hot day.

The mule looks thirsty.

Koko: Are you thirsty?

(Then, Koko's mom shouts.)

Mom: Wake up, Koko! Drink your orange juice with ice cubes!

Koko: Mule, do you want some orange juice with ice cubes...?

Mom: Wake up, Koko! It's time to go to your flute lesson!

Koko: Mule...it's time to go to your flute lesson...

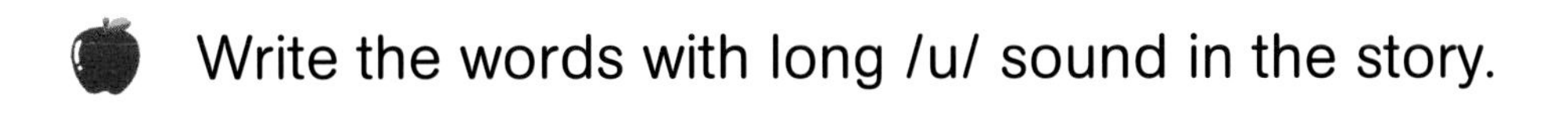

Write the words with long /u/ sound in the story.

Unit 6

L-blend
bl, cl, gl, pl

This is Emma's classroom. She goes to school early today.

bl-
cl-
gl-
pl-

black

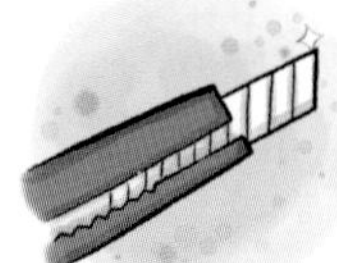
blade

class-
room

clock

glass

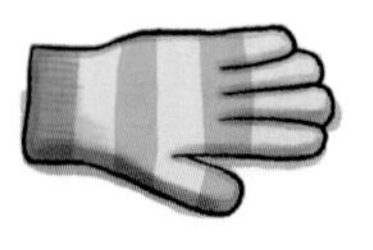
glove

plane

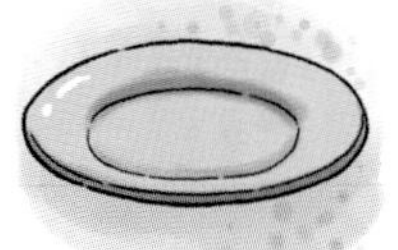
plate

plant

plum

Listen, Repeat and Write

track 07

bl- cl-
gl- pl-

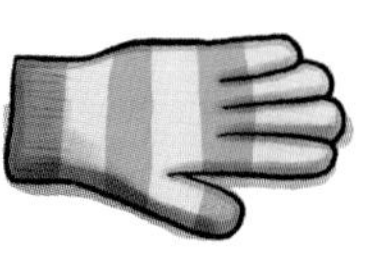

glove

clock

classroom

plant

black

glass

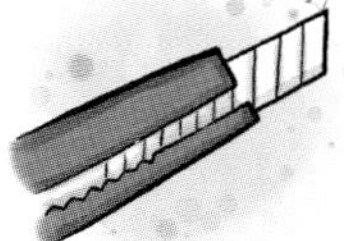

blade

plum

plane

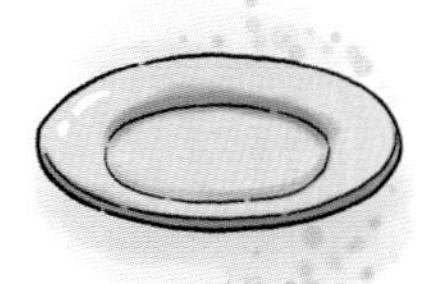

plate

Listen and Circle

1.

2.

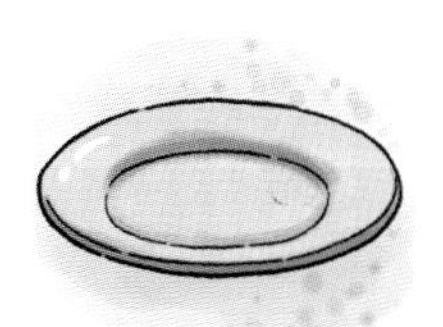

Listen, Check and Match

1. 

Ⓐ Ⓑ

2. 

Ⓐ Ⓑ

3. 

Ⓐ Ⓑ

4. 

Ⓐ Ⓑ

Listen and Fill in the blanks

1. There is a  ____________ board in the  ____________.

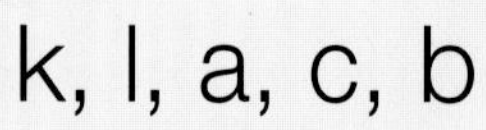

a, s, c, o, m, o, l, s, r

2. Emma drops  ____________s on a 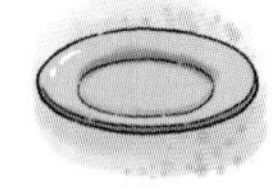 ____________.

m, p, u, l

a, e, t, p, l

3. Look at the  ____________ and the  ____________

v, l, o, e, g

k, l, c, o, c

on the street.

Listen, Read and Play

It was Koko's first day of school.

Koko comes home and sits with her mom.

Mom: How was school?

Koko: It was great, mom. I did many things!

Mom: Really? Tell me more, Koko.

Koko: I wrote on the blackboard. I wrote on my desk.

I broke the classroom clock.

And I ate all the plums from the plum tree!

Mom: Oh...no, Koko.

Write the words with /bl/, /cl/, /gl/ and /pl/ sound in the story.

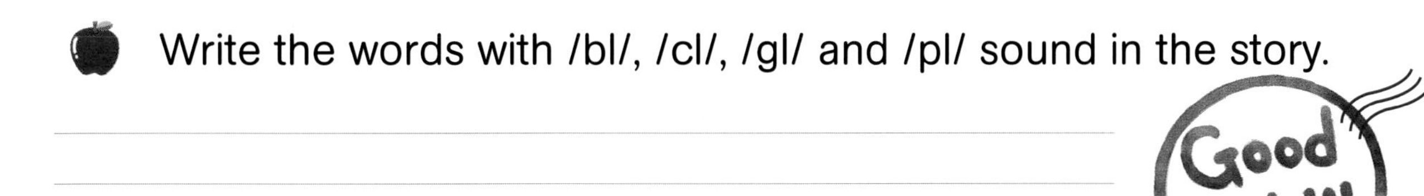

1 Listen and write the letter.  

d m

s t

ass

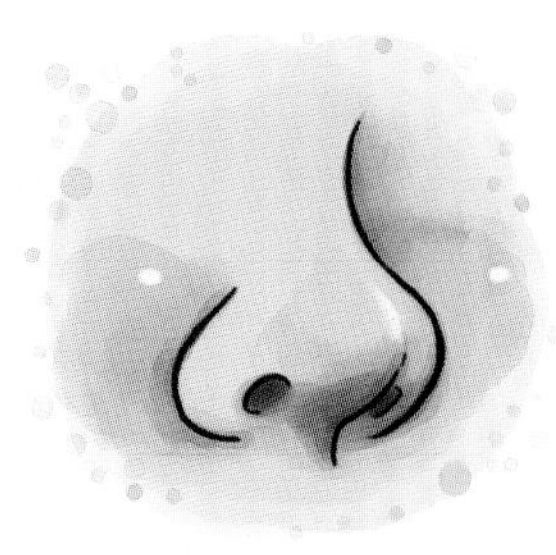

n s

j ce

ane

 Listen and circle the correct word. 

hape
hope
hepe

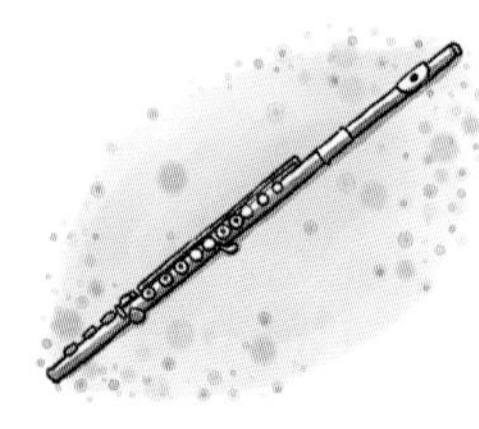

flate
flote
flute

black
block
bluck

hame
hume
home

Jone
June
Jane

clack
clock
cluck

 Connect and write.

	c		ule	______
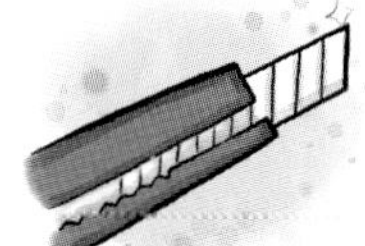	b		one	______
	m		um	______
	pl		lade	______
	c		ole	______
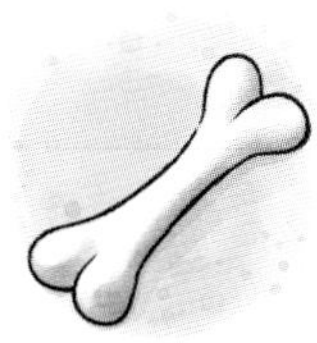	b		ate	______
	m		ube	______
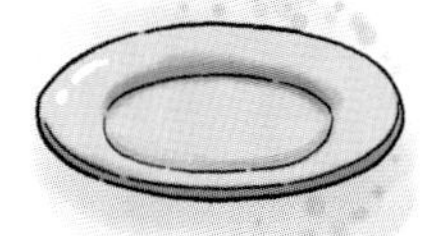	pl		one	______

4 Listen and fill in the blanks.

1. Bobo: Look! There is a h____l____.

   Koko: Oh no! Let's cover the h____l____ with dirt!

   Bobo: Oh wait. Look! I see a n____s____!

   Koko: It's a m____l____!

   Bobo: The h____l____ is a m____l____'s h____m____!

2. Koko has a dream about a m____l____.

   The mule is on a d____n____.

   It is a very hot day.

   The m____l____ looks thirsty.

3. Mom: How was school?

   Koko: It was great, mom. I did many things!

   Mom: Really? Tell me more, Koko.

   Koko: I wrote on the ____ ____ackboard. I wrote on my desk.

   I broke the ____ ____assroom ____ ____ock.

   And I ate all the ____ ____ums from the ____ ____um tree!

   Mom: Oh…no, Koko.

Let's Play A Game

Play tic-tac-toe game with your partner.

How to Play:

1. Choose a square.
2. Say the name of the picture that you chose. Then, complete the word.
3. When you complete the word, put a check mark on the picture. If you can't, do not put a check mark.
4. Take turns choosing squares and continue the game.
5. The one who gets four in a row wins.

R-blend
br, dr, pr, tr

Emma and Willy are at a toy shop on Nexus street.

br-
dr-
pr-
tr-

	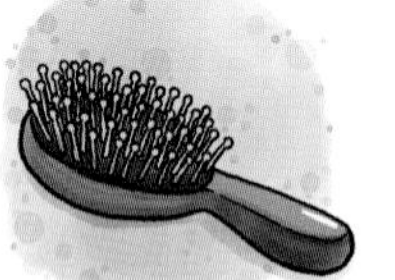			
bread	brush	brick	bride	dress

drum	price	prince	train	truck

Listen, Repeat and Write

br- dr-
pr- tr-

price

prince

bread

train

dress

drum

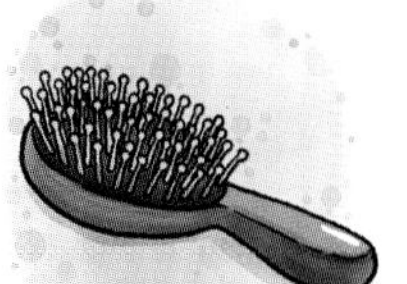

brush

truck

bride

brick

Listen and Circle

1.

2.

Listen, Check and Match 

1. 

Ⓐ Ⓑ

2. prince
Ⓐ Ⓑ

3. 

Ⓐ Ⓑ

4. 

Listen and Fill in the blanks 

1. The 

__________ of the  __________ is 2, 000 won.

i, r, c, e, p   e, d, r, b, a

2. Put your toy  __________s and 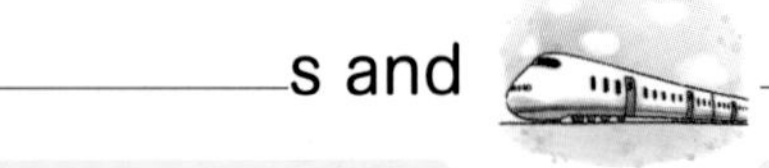 __________s away.

r, k, c, u, t   r, i, a, n, t

3. The  __________ in a white  __________ is beautiful.

b, i, d, e, r   e, s, r, d, s

Listen, Read and Play

Koko and Bobo are at a toyshop.

There are lots of toys.

Koko: Look! It's a doll with a bride's dress!

(Bobo plays the drum. He can't hear Koko.)

Do you want to brush her hair, Bobo?

Bobo: What? No! I don't want to play with the truck and the train.

Koko: No-no. Do you want to play with my doll?

Bobo: What? No! I don't want to play with the door!

Write the words with /br/, /dr/, /pr/ and /tr/ sound in the story.

Good Job!!!

Unit 8 S-blend sm, sn, sp, st

Emma and Willy are in a ghost house. It is dark and scary.

sm-
sn-
sp-
st-

smell smile snail snake spider

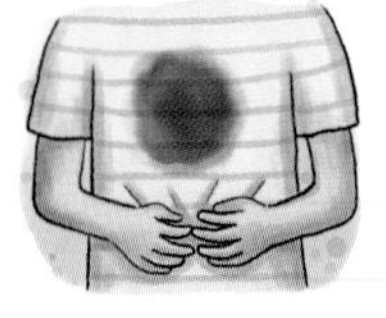  

spot stone stop store stove

Listen, Repeat and Write  

sm- sn- sp- st-

spot

spider

snake

store

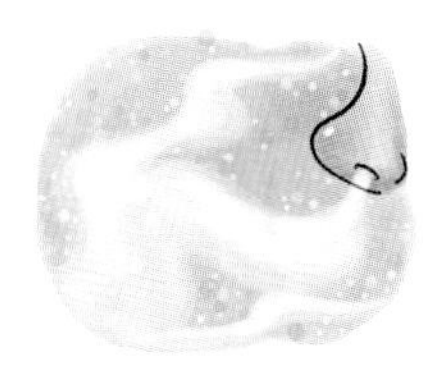

smell

snail

stove

smile

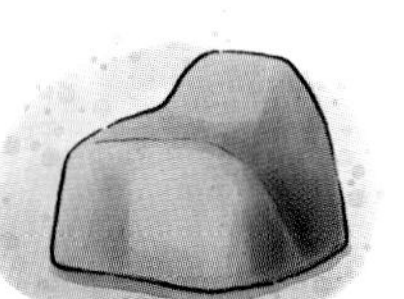

stone

stop

Listen and Circle 

1.

 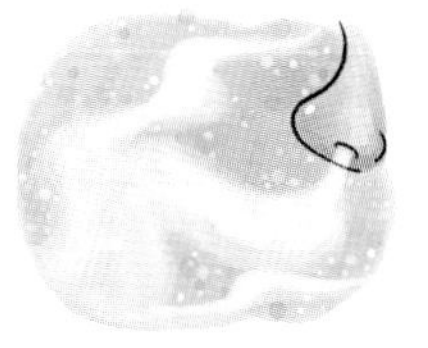

2.

Listen, Check and Match 

1. smile

Ⓐ Ⓑ

2. 

Ⓐ Ⓑ

3. 

Ⓐ Ⓑ

4. 

Ⓐ Ⓑ

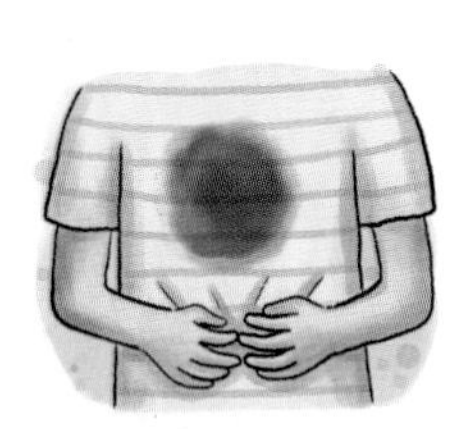

Listen and Fill in the blanks 

1. There is a  ______________ on an old 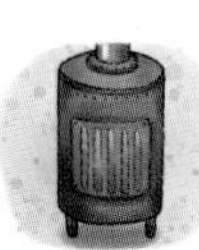 ______________.

s, e, d, i, p, r　　　o, t, e, v, s

2. Look at the  ______________ behind the 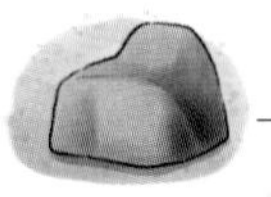 ______________.

a, k, s, n, e　　　o, e, t, n, s

3. Emma 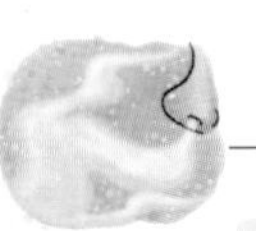 ______________s the roses at a flower  ______________.

e, l, l, m, s　　　o, t, r, e, s

Listen, Read and Play

Koko and Bobo are in a cave.

It is dark and scary inside the cave.

Koko: Bobo, it smells bad. I'm scared.

Bobo: Haha. Don't worry. I am strong and brave!

Koko: Oh Bobo! There's a snake by the stone.

Bobo: Haha. Don't worry.

Koko: Oh no! Bobo, there's a spider on your back!

Bobo: Ahhh! Where? Help me!

Write the words with /sm/, /sn/, /sp/ and /st/ sound in the story.

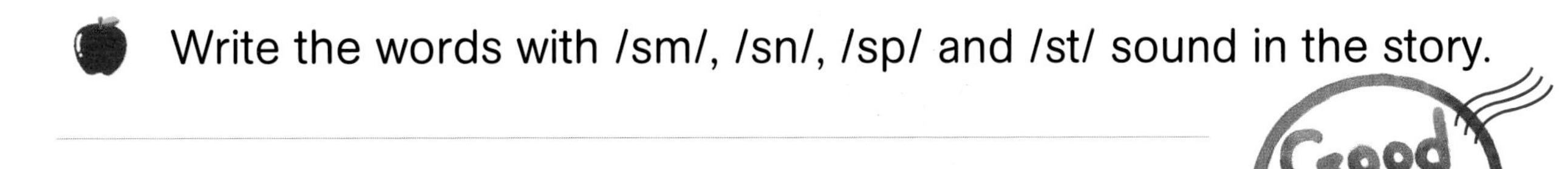

Good Job!!!

Ending-blend nd, ng, nk, nt

Emma's family goes camping in the woods.

-nd
-ng
-nk
-nt

land

pond

sing

wing

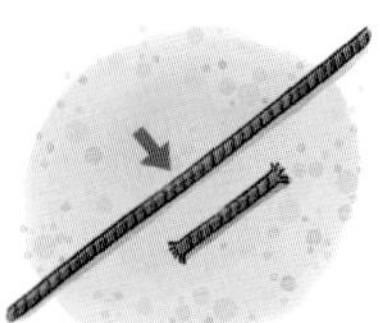
long

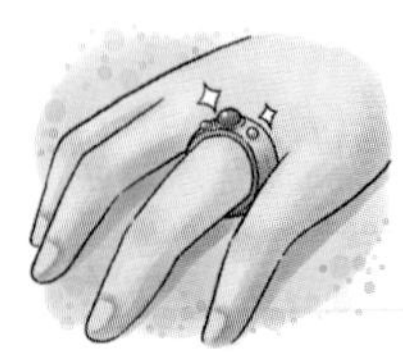
ring

drink

wink

ant

tent

Listen, Repeat and Write  track 11

-nd -ng
-nk -nt

drink

wink

land

wing

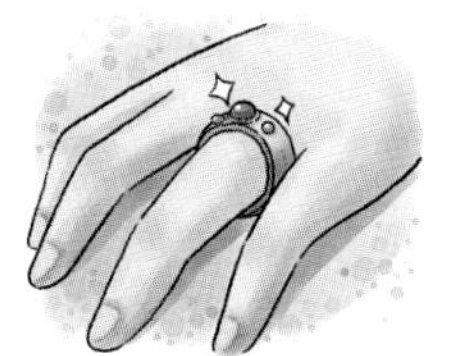

ring

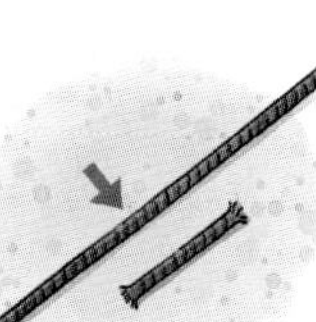

long

pond

sing

tent

ant

Listen and Circle 

1.

2.

Listen, Check and Match 

1. sing Ⓐ Ⓑ
2. wink Ⓐ Ⓑ
3. land Ⓐ Ⓑ
4. ring Ⓐ Ⓑ

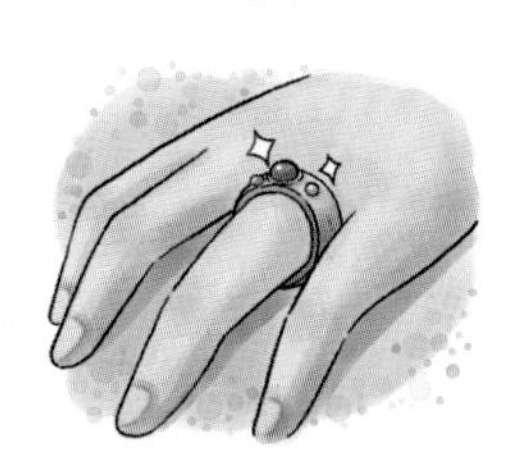   

Listen and Fill in the blanks 

1. An  ____________ does not have  ____________s.

   t, n, a　　　　i, g, w, n

2. Emma is  ____________ing water in a  ____________.

   r, n, d, i, k　　　　n, t, e, t

3. Emma drops a 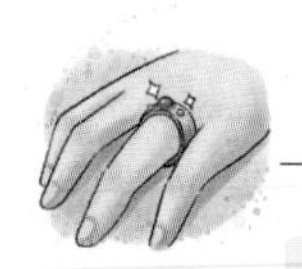 ____________ in a 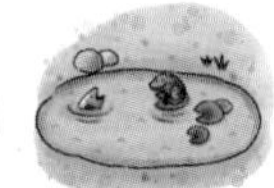 ____________.

   n, r, i, g　　　　n, d, p, o

Listen, Read and Play

Koko and her dad are camping in the woods by the pond.

They make the tent and sit by a small pond.

Koko is happy, and she sings. Koko's dad points to an ant.

Dad: Look, Koko! There's an ant in the pond!

Koko: Oh no! Can it swim?

Dad: No, but a queen ant has wings. So, it's okay.

Koko: Oh, but its wings are wet, dad!

Dad: Hmmm. Let's give the ant a leaf.

Koko: Look! It got on the leaf! It's safe now!

Write the words with /nd/, /ng/, /nk/ and /nt/ sound in the story.

Good Job!!!

1 Listen and write the letter.

ick

ile

si

um

op

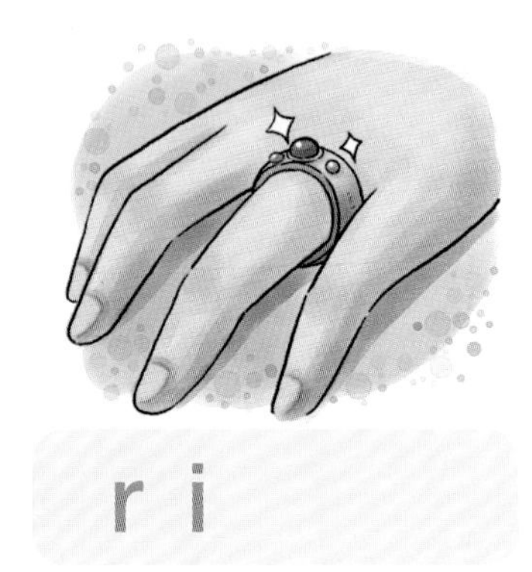

ri

2 Listen and circle the correct word.

brush
drush
prush

smail
snail
spail

land
lang
lank

brince
drince
prince

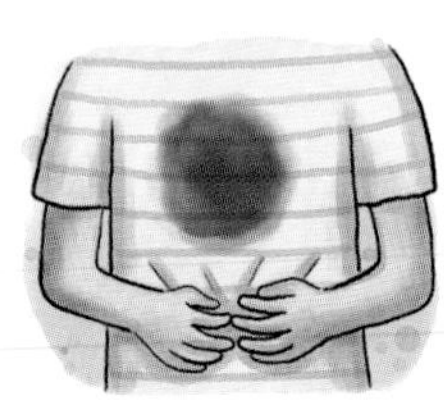

snot
smot
spot

wind
wing
wink

3 Connect and write.

	d	rain	______
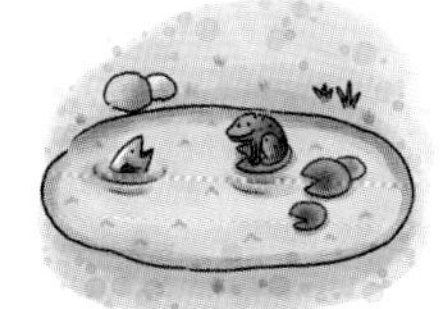	p	mell	______
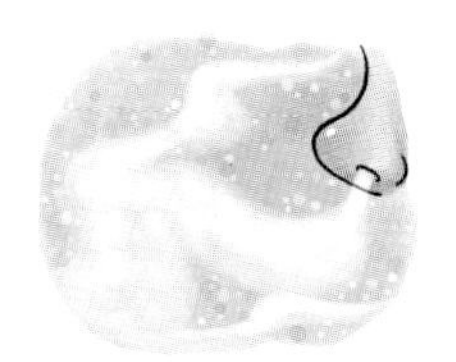	s	ress	______
	t	ond	______
	d	rince	______
	p	rink	______
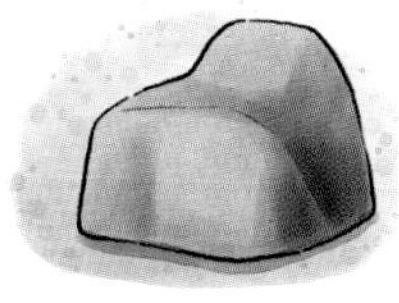	s	ent	______
	t	tone	______

4 Listen and fill in the blanks. 

1. Koko: Look! It's a doll with a ____ ____ide's ____ ____ess!

   (Bobo plays the ____ ____um. He can't hear Koko.)

   Do you want to ____ ____ush her hair, Bobo?

   Bobo: What? No! I don't want to play with the ____ ____uck and the ____ ____ain.

   Koko: No-no. Do you want to play with my doll?

   Bobo: What? No! I don't want to play with the door!

2. Koko: Bobo, It ____ ____ells bad. I'm scared.

   Bobo: Haha. Don't worry. I am strong and brave!

   Koko: Oh Bobo! There's a ____ ____ake by the ____ ____one.

   Bobo: Haha. Don't worry.

   Koko: Oh no! Bobo, there's a ____ ____ider on your back!

   Bobo: Ahhh! Where? Help me!

3. Koko and her dad are camping in the woods by the po____ ____.

   They make the te____ ____ and sit by a small po____ ____.

   Koko is happy, and she si____ ____s.

   Koko's dad points to an a____ ____.

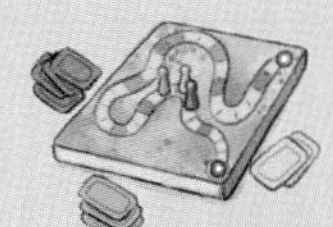

Let's Play A Game

Play a board game with your partner. You need picture cards(C set).

sn-	pr-	-nd	tr-		st-	-ng
	-nk	br-	sp-	-ng	dr-	pr-
dr-	sp-	sm-	-nd	st-	-ng	
-nt	tr-		sn-	dr-	-nk	-nt
sn-	-nk	sp-		sm-	pr-	br-

How to Play:

1. Spread the picture cards around the board and place a coin in a corner.
2. Flick the coin and sound out the letter where the coin lands on.
3. Take a matching picture card and speak out what is on the picture like "br-bread."
4. The winner is the one who gets the most cards.

Digraph ch, ph, sh, th, wh

Willy takes a bath. He plays with his toys in a bathtub.

ch-
ph-
sh-
th-
wh-

chair cheese phone photo shell

ship thirteen thumb whale white

Listen, Repeat and Write

 track 13

ch-
ph- sh-
th- wh-

thirteen

thumb

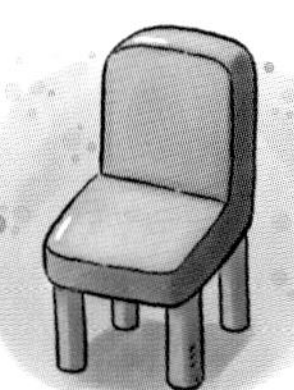

chair

phone

whale

white

cheese

photo

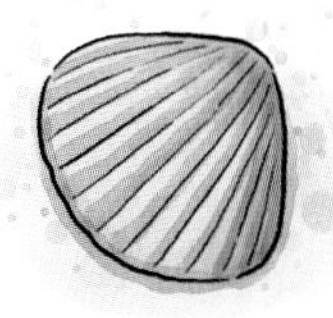

ship

shell

Listen and Circle

1.

2.

Listen, Check and Match 

1. 

Ⓐ Ⓑ

2. 

Ⓐ Ⓑ

3. 

Ⓐ Ⓑ

4. 

Ⓐ Ⓑ

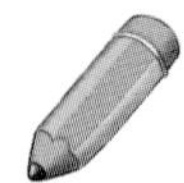

Listen and Fill in the blanks 

1. Look at the  ____________  ____________ over there.

h, e, t, w, i　　o, h, p, e, n

2. There are  ____________  ____________s in the classroom.

t, i, r, e, h, e, n, t　　c, i, a, r, h

3. Do not throw the toy  ____________ or  ____________ in the sea.

h, s, p, i　　h, e, s, e, c, e

Listen, Read and Play

Koko meets her sea friends.

A shell and a white whale sit in their chairs.

Shell: Koko, I want to visit your house.

Koko: Sure, but how can we go?

Whale: Hmmm... We can take the ship!

Shell: How long will it take? What do we eat?

Koko: It will take thirteen days!

And I have some cheese in my pocket. We can eat cheese!

Shell and Whale: Thirteen days with only cheese? No way!

Write the words with /ch/, /ph/, /sh/, /th/ and /wh/ sound in the story.

____

____

____

Good Job!!!

Double Letter Vowels oa, ow

This is Emma's room. She is going outside.

boat

coat

goat

soap

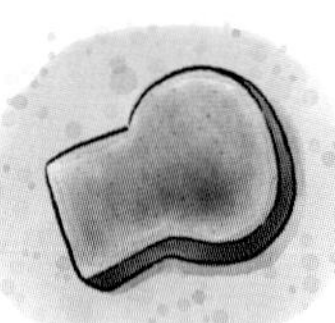
toast

bowl

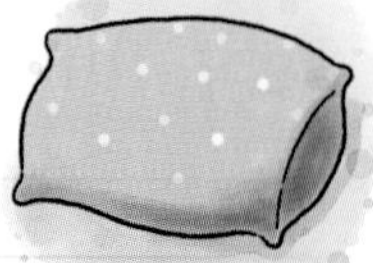
pillow

snow

window

yellow

Listen, Repeat and Write

 track 14

-oa-
-ow

window

toast

bowl

boat

pillow

snow

yellow

coat

goat

soap

Listen and Circle

1.

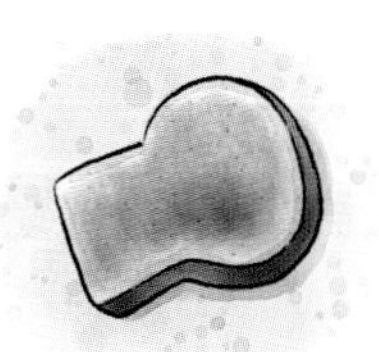

2.

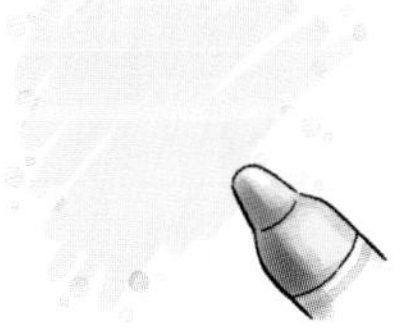

Listen, Check and Match 

1. 

Ⓐ Ⓑ

2. 

Ⓐ Ⓑ

3. 

Ⓐ Ⓑ

4. 

Ⓐ Ⓑ

Listen and Fill in the blanks 

1. The  ______________ (o, l, w, e, y, l) ______________ (a, c, o, t) is outside the closet.

2. Have  ______________ (s, o, t, a, t) and a  ______________ (o, l, b, w) of soup.

3. Look! A  ______________ (a, g, o, t) is on the  ______________ (t, o, b, a).

Listen, Read and Play

Bobo comes over to Koko's house. Bobo wants to play outside in the snow.

But, Koko cannot find her hairbrush!

Koko: Is it next to the toy boat?

Bobo: No, it's not here!

Koko: Then, is it behind the toy goat?

Bobo: No, it's not there!

Koko: Look under the yellow pillow, Bobo!

Bobo: No, it's not here. Oh wait! It's on the bed!

Koko: Ah-ha! Great! Now, let's go play outside!

Bobo: But... what about your room? It's very dirty.

Write the words with /oa/ and /ow/ sound in the story.

____

____

____

Double Letter Vowels
oi, oy

Willy and Emma are in a playroom at a toy shop.

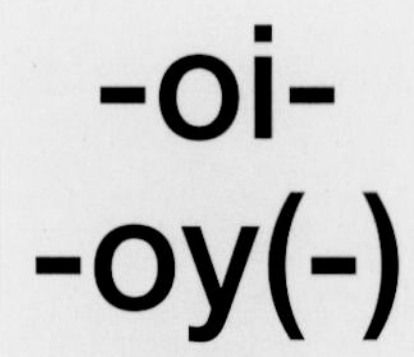

		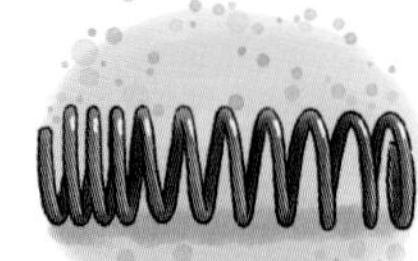		
boil	soil	coil	coin	point

toilet	boy	joy	toy	oyster

Listen, Repeat and Write

track 15

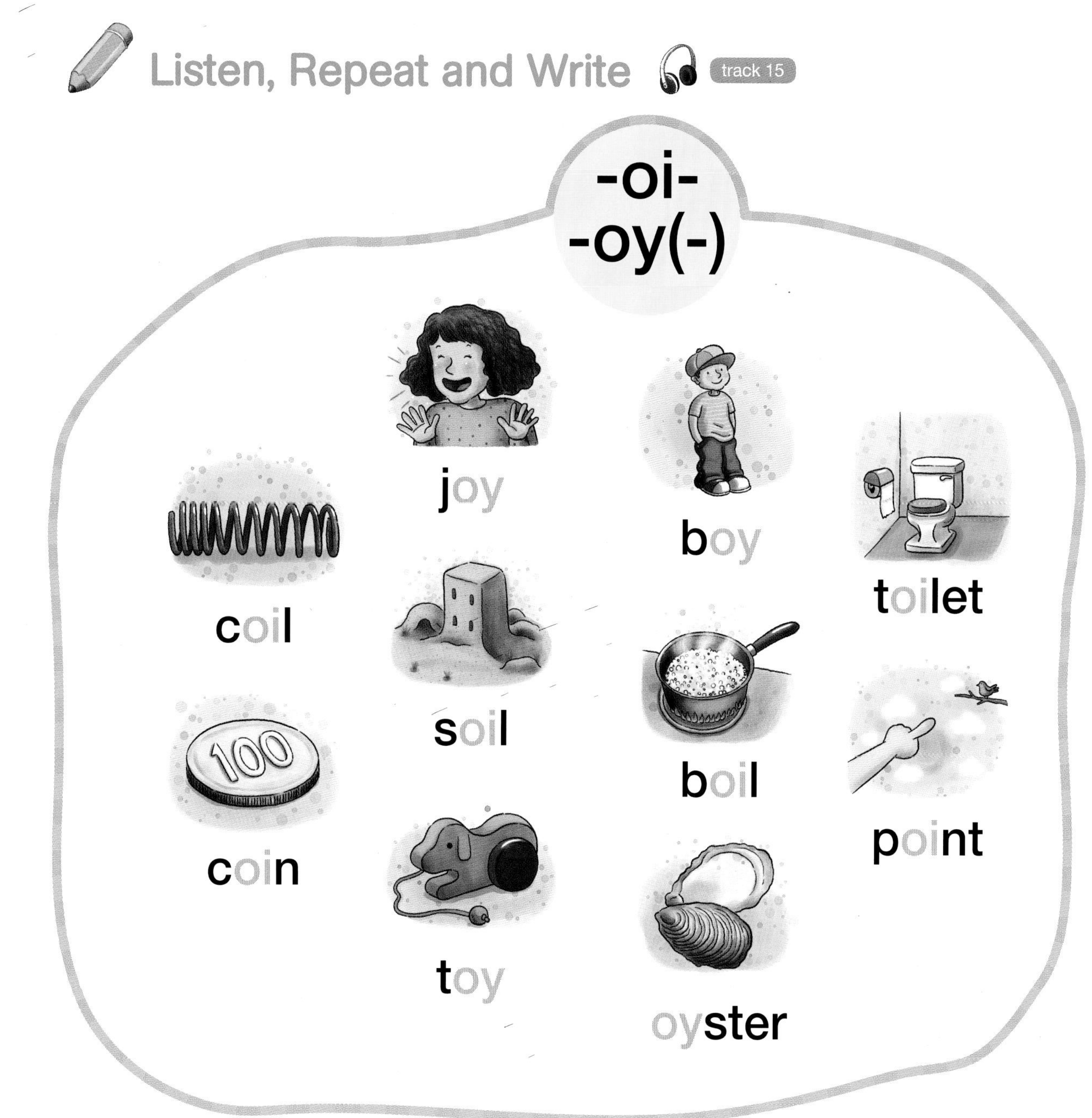

Listen and Circle

1.

2.

Listen, Check and Match 

1. 

Ⓐ Ⓑ

2. 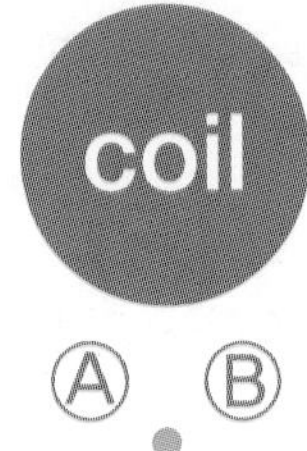

Ⓐ Ⓑ

3. 

Ⓐ Ⓑ

4. 

  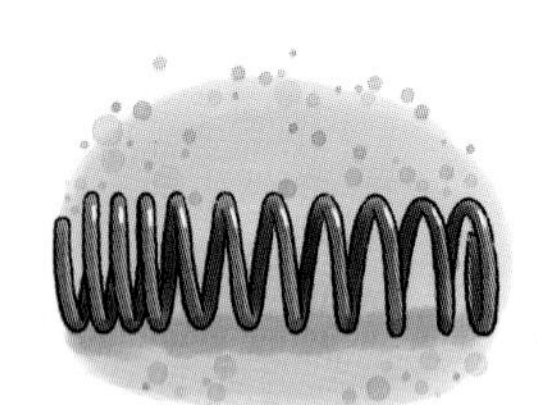 

Listen and Fill in the blanks 

1. A  ________  ________s an egg.

y, b, o　　l, o, b, i

2. Emma goes to the  ________ with a  ________.

e, t, o, l, i, t　　y, o, t

3. There are a  ________ and an  ________.

i, o, c, n　　s, e, r, t, o, y

Listen, Read and Play

Bobo wants to play in the sandbox.

But a boy is there. He's making a sandcastle.

Bobo: Can I play with you?

Boy: No. Go away.

Bobo: I will give you that toy.

(Bobo points to a toy airplane.)

Boy: No, I don't like airplanes.

(Then, a coin drops from Bobo's hand.)

Boy: Oooh! A coin! I will give you my sandcastle. I want this coin!

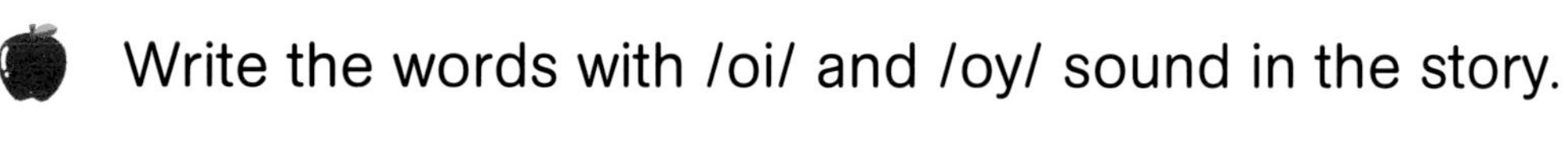

Write the words with /oi/ and /oy/ sound in the story.

1 Listen and write the letter.  

i p	wind	p nt

oto	s l	j

 Listen and circle the correct word. 

	chell shell phell		pilloa pillow pilloy	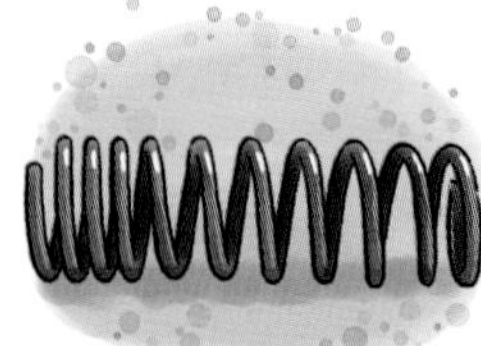	coil coal coy
	shale thale whale		chair shair whair		coat cout coy

 Connect and write.

	b	humb	______
	c	heese	______
	s	oap	______
	t	oat	______
	b	oin	______
	c	oil	______
	s	now	______
	t	oilet	______

 Listen and fill in the blanks. 

1. Koko meets her sea friends.

   A _____ _____ell and a _____ _____ite _____ _____ale sit in their _____ _____airs.

   Shell: Koko, I want to visit your house.

   Koko: Sure, but how can we go?

   Whale: Hmmm... We can take the _____ _____ip!

2. Koko: Is it next to the toy b_____ _____t?

   Bobo: No, it's not here!

   Koko: Then, is it behind the toy g_____ _____t?

   Bobo: No, it's not there!

   Koko: Look under the yell_____ _____ pill_____ _____, Bobo!

   Bobo: No, it's not here. Oh wait! It's on the bed!

3. Bobo: I will give you that t_____ _____.

   (Bobo p_____ _____nts to a t_____ _____ airplane.)

   Boy: No, I don't like airplanes.

   (Then, a c_____ _____n drops from Bobo's hand.)

   Boy: Oooh! A c_____ _____n! I will give you my sandcastle. I want this

   c_____ _____n!

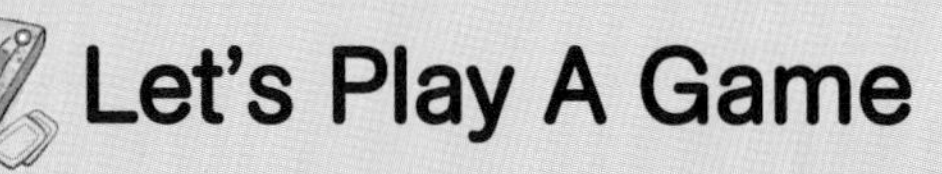

Let's Play A Game

Play a game with your partner.

How to Play:

1. Make word cards using the words that you learned in Unit 10, Unit 11, Unit 12.
2. Spread the word cards that you made on the desk.
3. A teacher chooses a flash card randomly. Then the teacher reads the card out loud.
4. Listen to the word your teacher says. Then try to be the first student to touch the correct word card. The first student takes the word card.
5. The student who gets the most scores wins.

Double Letter Vowels
ou, ow

After the party, Emma and Willy are on the way home.

-ou-
-ow-

cloud

loud

house

mouth

cow

owl

gown

crown

brown

clown

Listen, Repeat and Write  track 17

-ou-
-ow-

cow

owl

brown

gown

house

clown

crown

mouth

cloud

loud

Listen and Circle 

1.

2.

Listen, Check and Match 

1. 

Ⓐ Ⓑ

2. 

Ⓐ Ⓑ

3. 

Ⓐ Ⓑ

4. 

Ⓐ Ⓑ

Listen and Fill in the blanks 

1. A  ____________ goes into his  ____________.

l, w, n, o, c　　　　u, s, o, h, e

2. Willy in a  ____________ speaks  ____________er.

w, g, o, n　　　　d, o, l, u

3. There are a  ____________ and an  ____________ near a pine tree.

w, o, c

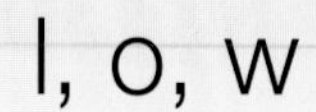

Listen, Read and Play

It is Halloween! Everyone dressed up for Halloween!

Koko is wearing a brown gown and a crown. She looks like a queen.

Bobo: Koko, you look pretty!

Koko: Bobo, thank you! You are a very handsome clown, too!

Bobo: Haha. Thanks, Koko.

Emma: What about me?

Koko: Oh, sorry, Emma. You are a very cute owl!

Emma: Koo. Koo. I sound like an owl, too!

Write the words with /ou/ and /ow/ sound in the story.

Double Letter Vowels
er, ir, ur

Emma thinks what she wants to do in the future.

-er
-ir-
-ur-

letter

singer

farmer

teacher

bird

girl

shirt

skirt

nurse

purse

Listen, Repeat and Write

track 18

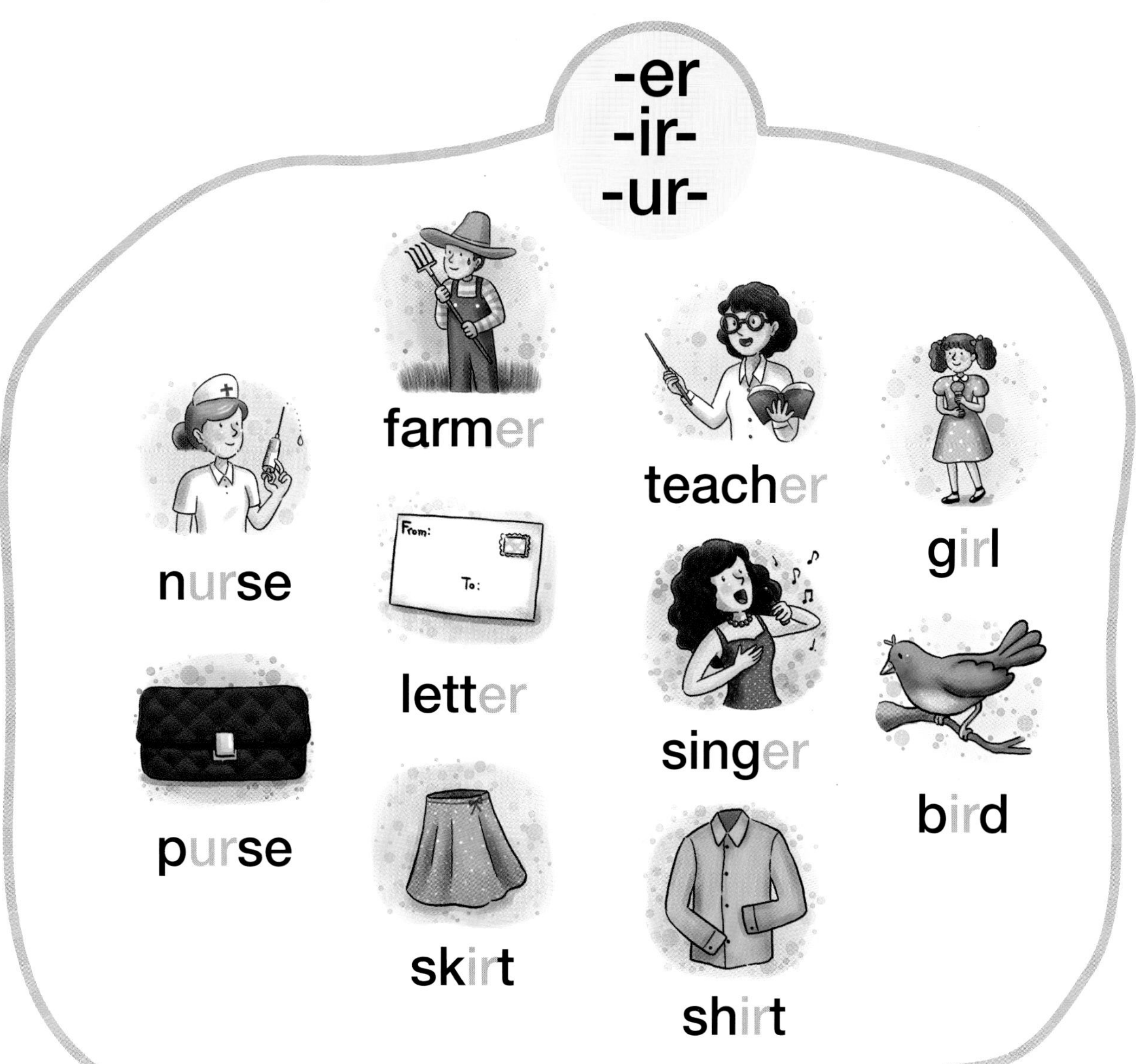

Listen and Circle

1.

2.

Listen, Check and Match

1. 

Ⓐ Ⓑ

2. 

Ⓐ Ⓑ

3. 

Ⓐ Ⓑ

4. 

Ⓐ Ⓑ

Listen and Fill in the blanks

1. A  ______________ wears a  ______________.

r, l, g, i   r, k, i, s, t

2. A  ______________ is writing a  ______________.

t, e, c, e, a, r, h   t, e, r, e, t, l

3. A  ______________ wants to buy a  ______________.

n, e, s, i, r, g   u, s, p, e, r

Listen, Read and Play

Koko waits for the bus at the bus stop.

A nurse, a boy in a shirt and a girl in a skirt are at the bus stop.

Nurse: Excuse me, what time is it?

Koko: Sorry, I don't know.

Boy: Excuse me, what time is it?

Koko: Sorry, I don't know.

Girl: Excuse me. You have a watch. Please tell us what time it is.

Koko: Ohhh! It's a toy watch. It's not a real watch!

Write the words with /er/, /ir/ and /ur/ sound in the story.

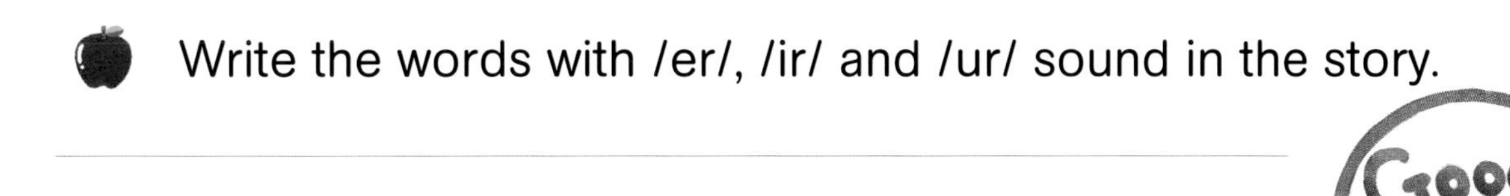

Good Job!!!

Double Letter Vowels oo

One evening, Emma cooks some food for her mom.

book

cook

food

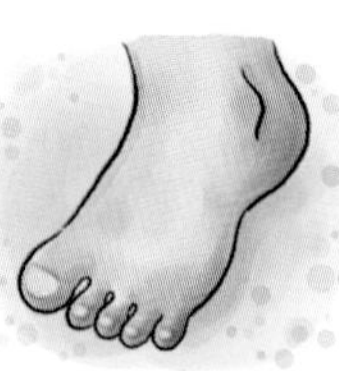

foot

goose

moon

pool

spoon

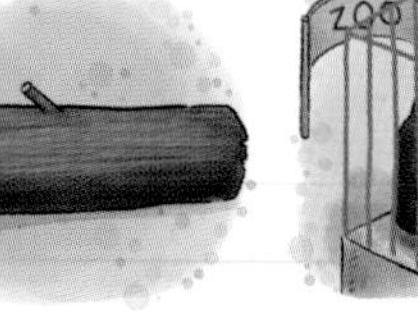

wood

zoo

Listen, Repeat and Write  track 19

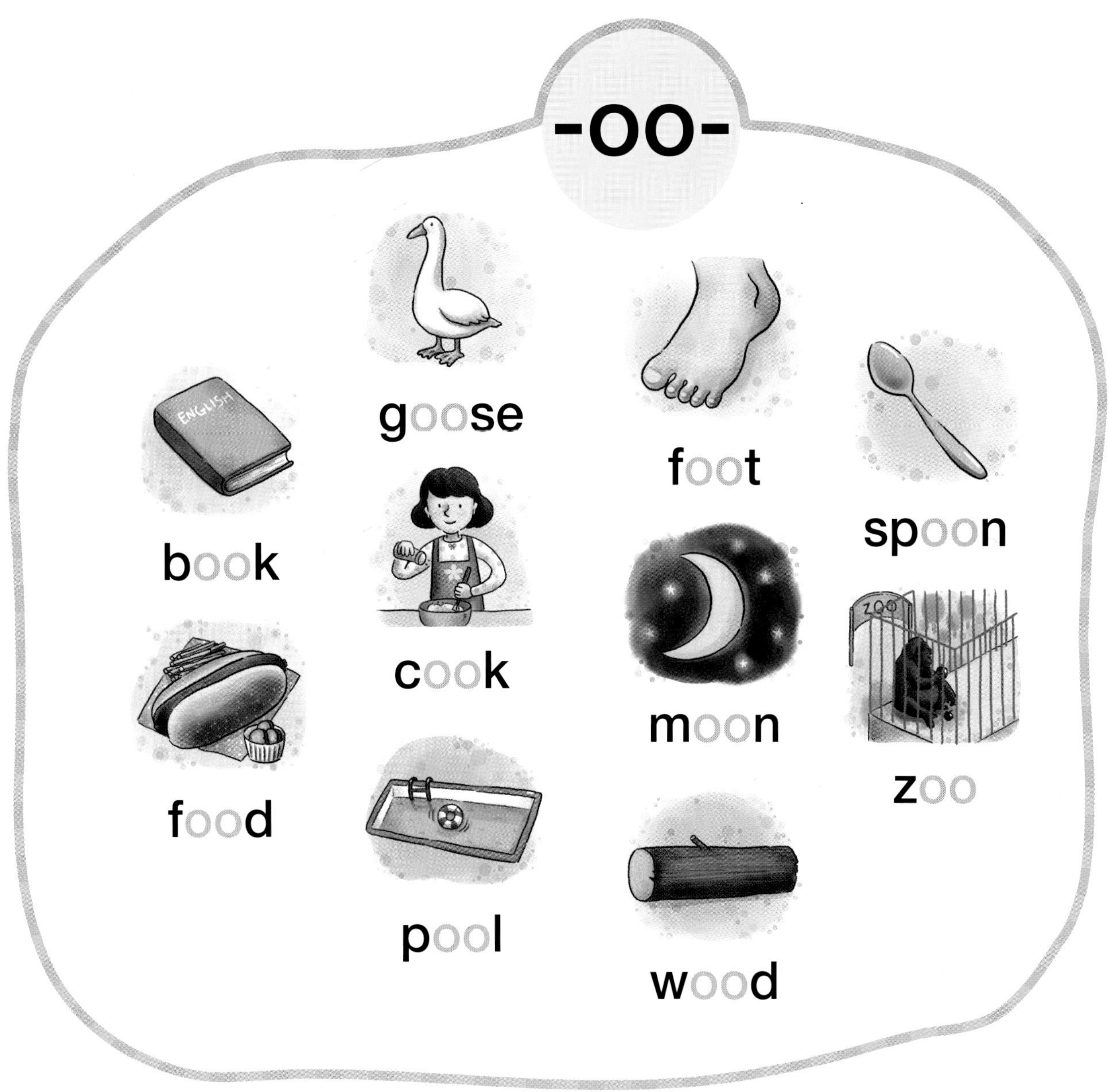

Listen and Circle 

1.

2.

Listen, Check and Match 

1. 

Ⓐ Ⓑ

2. 

Ⓐ Ⓑ

3. 

Ⓐ Ⓑ

4. 

Ⓐ Ⓑ

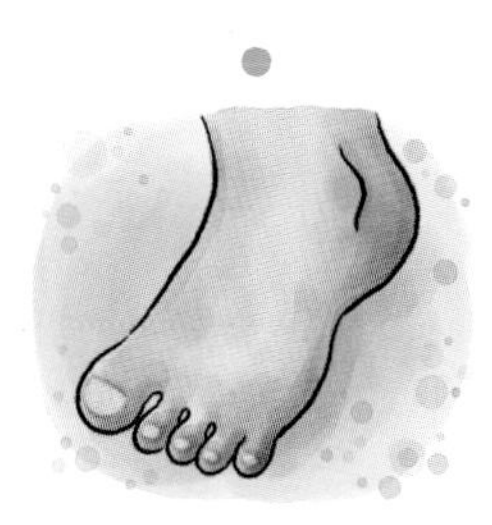

Listen and Fill in the blanks 

1. There are  ______________ (d, o, o, f) and  ______________s (o, s, n, o, p) on the table.

2. Emma sees a  ______________ (s, o, e, g, o) at the  ______________ (o, o, z).

3. A  ______________ (k, o, b, o) store is next to a  ______________ (l, o, o, p).

Listen, Read and Play

Koko's school is going on a picnic to the zoo tomorrow.

Koko wants to cook some food for the picnic.

She takes out a cookbook and a wooden spoon.

Koko: I'm going to the zoo.

I'm going to see a goose.

Let's make some picnic food.

Let's make some sandwiches.

Yummy, yummy. Everyone will love my sandwich!

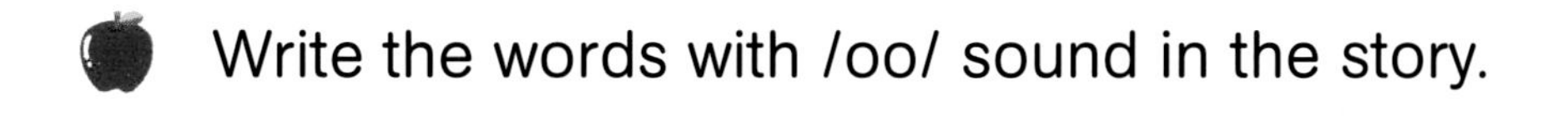

Write the words with /oo/ sound in the story.

1 Listen and write the letter.

2 Listen and circle the correct word.

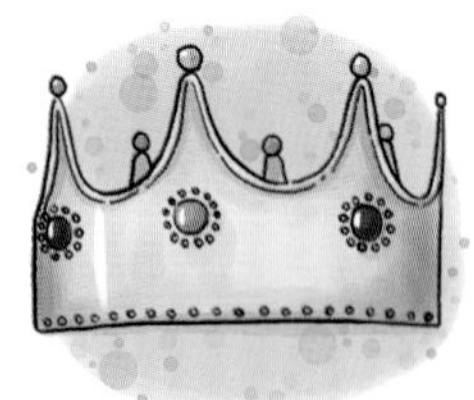

croun
crown
croan

mean
meen
moon

shert
shirt
shurt

broun
brown
broan

farmer
farmir
farmur

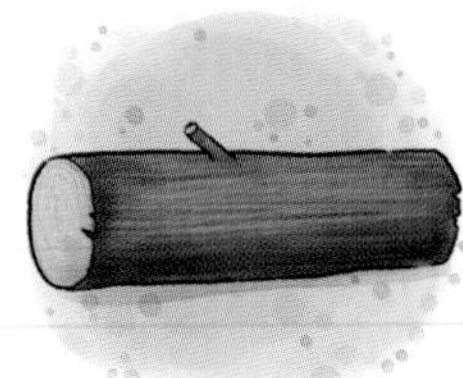

weed
wead
wood

 Connect and write.

Picture	Letter	Ending	Write
	b	oose	______
	g	kirt	______
	l	etter	______
	s	ook	______
	b	oud	______
	g	poon	______
	l	rown	______
	s	own	______

4 Listen and fill in the blanks. 

1. Everyone dressed up for Halloween!

   Koko is wearing a br____ ____n g____ ____n and a cr____ ____n.

   She looks like a queen.

   Bobo: Koko, you look pretty!

   Koko: Bobo, thank you! You are a very handsome cl____ ____n, too!

   Bobo: Haha. Thanks, Koko.

2. Koko waits for the bus at the bus stop.

   A n____ ____se, a boy in a sh____ ____t and a g____ ____l in a sk____ ____t are at the bus stop.

3. Koko's school is going on a picnic to the z____ ____ tomorrow.

   Koko wants to c____ ____k some f____ ____d for the picnic.

   She takes out a c____ ____kb____ ____k and a w____ ____den sp____ ____n.

   Koko: I'm going to the z____ ____. I'm going to see a g____ ____se.

   Let's make some picnic f____ ____d. Let's make some sandwiches. Yummy, yummy. Everyone will love my sandwich!

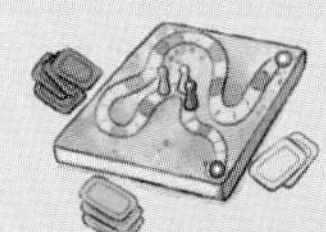

Let's Play A Game

Play a game with your partner.

How to Play:

1. Make a dice from the appendix.
2. Take turns throwing the dice.
3. Make a word that has the sound on the dice. For example, if your dice shows "ou", make a word that has "ou" sound like "cloud."
4. If you make a correct word, you get 5 points. If you can't, you lose 3 points.
5. The winner is the one who gets the most scores.

게임방법

Review (page 21)

준비물: 주사위, 그림 카드(A세트)

1. 주사위를 준비한다. 카드를 뒤집어 쌓아 놓는다.
2. 번갈아 가며 주사위를 던진다.
3. 주사위를 던진 다음 카드를 뽑아 영어로 똑바로 발음한다.
4. 제대로 발음을 하면 자신이 던진 주사위 숫자만큼 점수를 얻는다. 제대로 발음을 못하면 점수를 못 얻는다.
5. 점수를 제일 많이 얻은 사람이 승자이다.

Review (page 37)

준비물: 연필, 빙고판

1. 빙고판에 있는 그림 하나를 선택한 다음, 그림이 나타내는 단어를 영어로 말한다.
2. 그림을 영어로 말한 다음, 빈칸에 맞는 알파벳을 연필로 써서 단어를 완성한다.
3. 단어를 맞게 완성하면 그림에 체크를 한다. 그렇지 못하면 그림에 체크할 수 없다.
4. 번갈아 가며 그림을 선택하면서 게임을 계속 이어 간다.
5. 가로, 세로, 혹은 대각선으로 4열을 체크하면 이긴다.

Review (page 53)

준비물: 그림 카드(C세트), 동전

1. 게임판을 책상 위에 놓고 그림 카드를 게임판 주위에 잘 보이게 펼쳐 놓는다. 동전을 게임판 모퉁이 아무 데나 놓는다.
2. 동전을 튕겨 동전이 떨어진 곳의 글자를 보고 그 글자로 시작되는 단어 카드를 고른다.
3. 해당되는 그림 카드를 한 장 가져가며 소리와 단어를 말한다. (즉, 드레스 그림을 가져갈 경우 dr–dress라고 말한다.)
4. 그림 카드를 많이 모으는 사람이 승자가 된다. 참고로, 웃는 얼굴에 동전이 떨어지면 아무 카드나 가지고 갈 수 있고, 폭탄에 떨어지면 한 번을 쉬어야 한다.

Review (page 69)

준비물: 단어 카드

1. 먼저 학생들에게 11과, 12과, 13과에 나오는 단어를 종이에 써서 단어 카드를 만들게 한다.
2. 학생들이 만든 카드를 책상에 펼쳐 놓게 한다.
3. 선생님이 그림 카드를 보여 주며 단어를 말한다.
4. 선생님이 말하는 그림에 해당하는 단어 카드를 먼저 고르는 사람이 가져간다.
5. 카드를 제일 많이 가져간 사람이 승자이다.

Review (page 85)

준비물: 주사위

1. 부록으로 실린 주사위를 오려 만든다.
2. 돌아가면서 주사위를 던진다.
3. 던진 면이 나타내는 알파벳이 들어간 단어를 말한다.
4. 단어를 말하면 점수를 5점씩 얻는다. 올바른 단어를 만들지 못하면 3점씩 깎인다.
5. 점수를 제일 많이 얻은 사람이 승자이다.

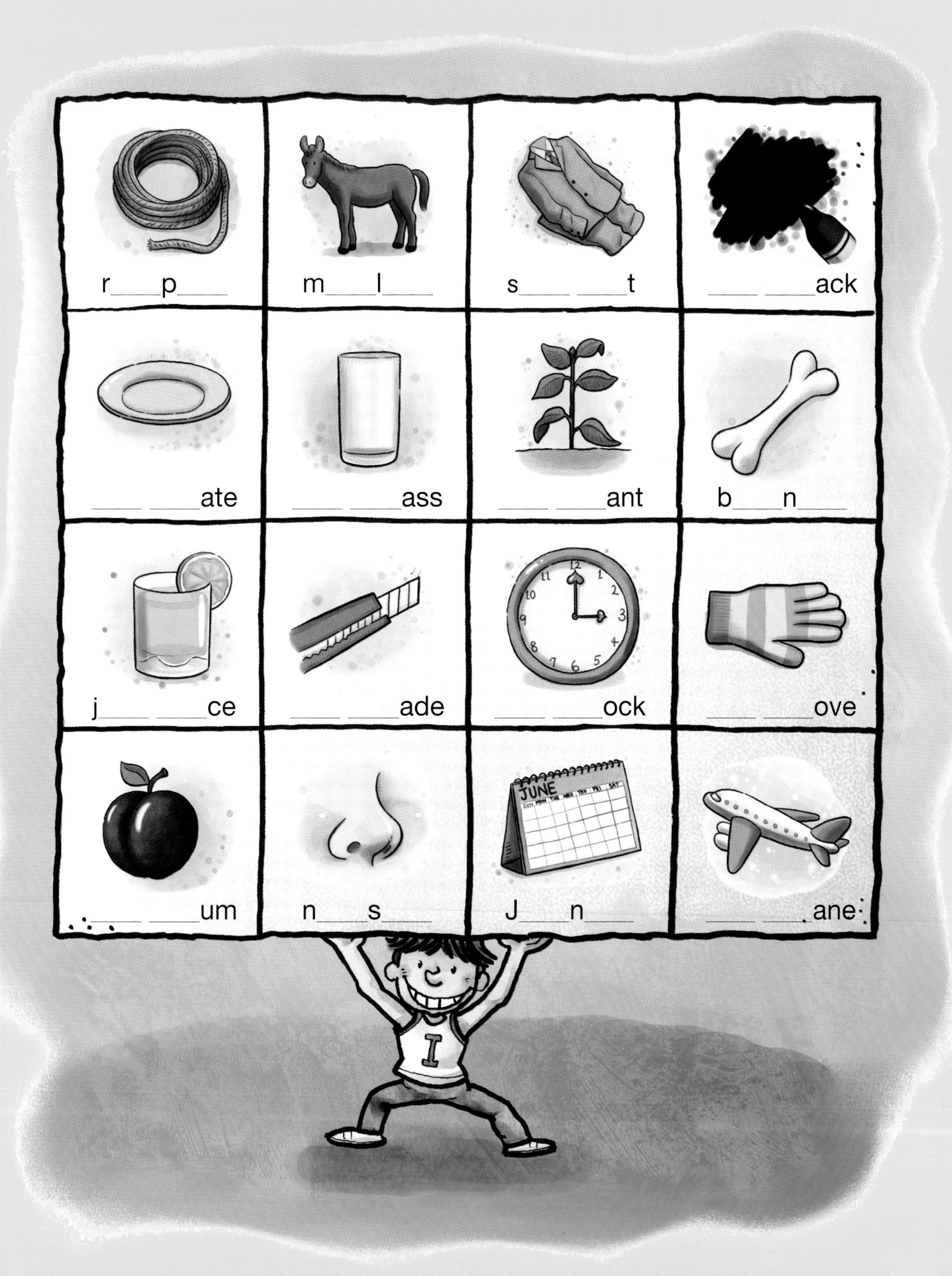
r___p___
m___l___
s___ ___t
___ ___ack
___ ___ate
___ ___ass
___ ___ant
b___n___
j___ ___ce
___ ___ade
___ ___ock
___ ___ove
___ ___um
n___s___
J___n___
___ ___ane
JUNE
SUN MON TUE WED THU FRI SAT

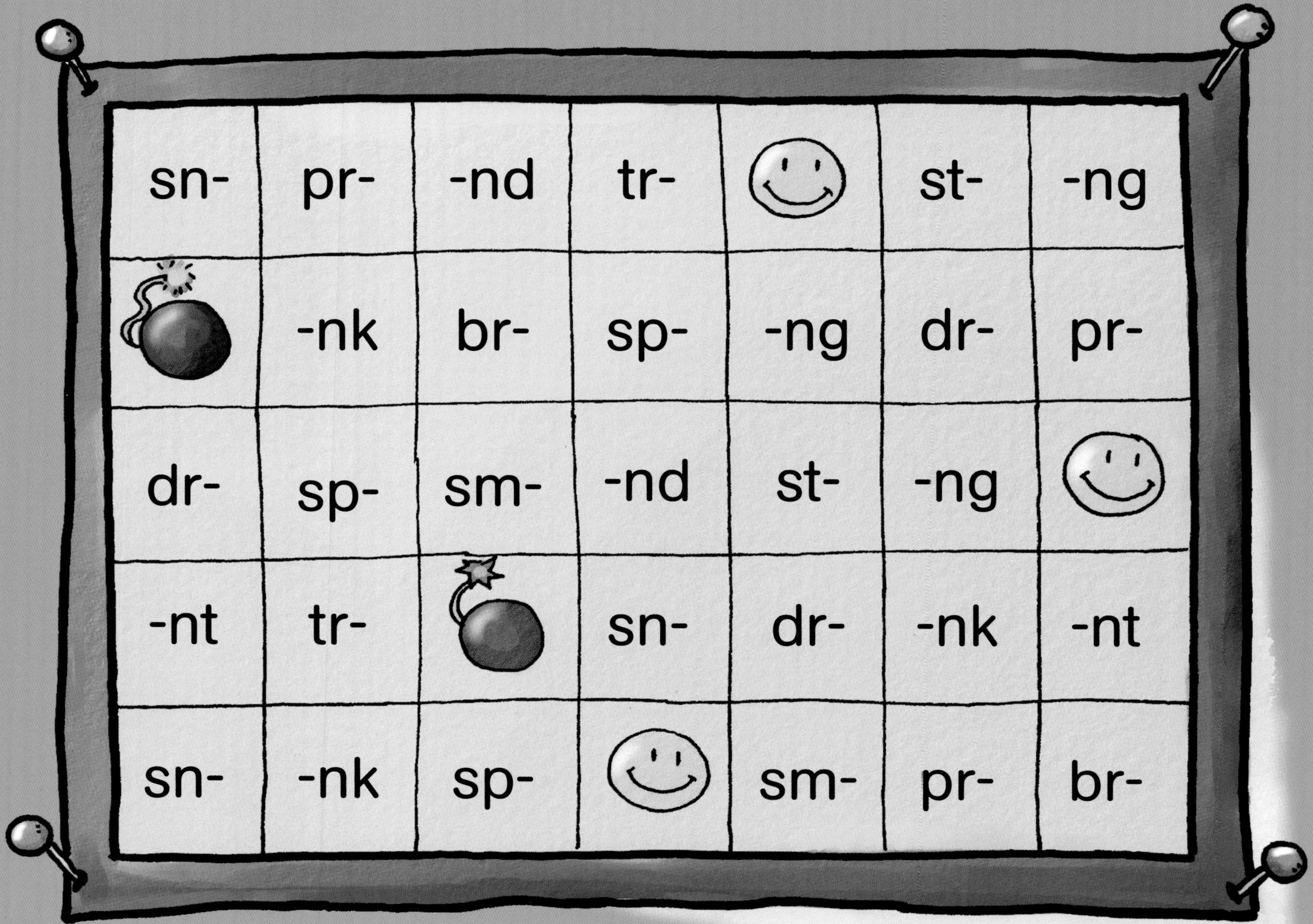

sn-	pr-	-nd	tr-		st-	-ng
	-nk	br-	sp-	-ng	dr-	pr-
dr-	sp-	sm-	-nd	st-	-ng	
-nt	tr-		sn-	dr-	-nk	-nt
sn-	-nk	sp-		sm-	pr-	br-

ou

ir oo ur

er

ow

3
7

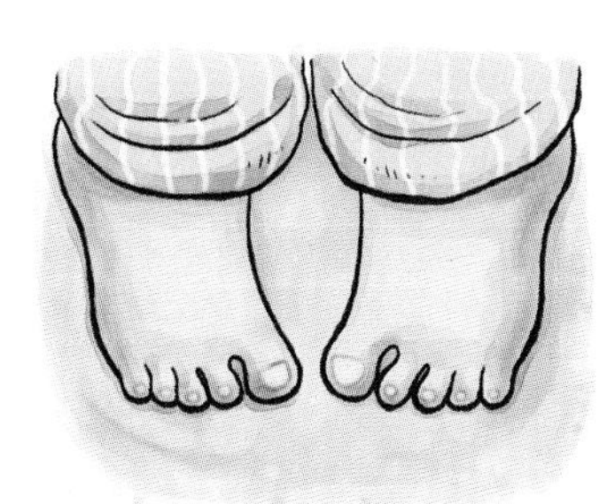

TEA

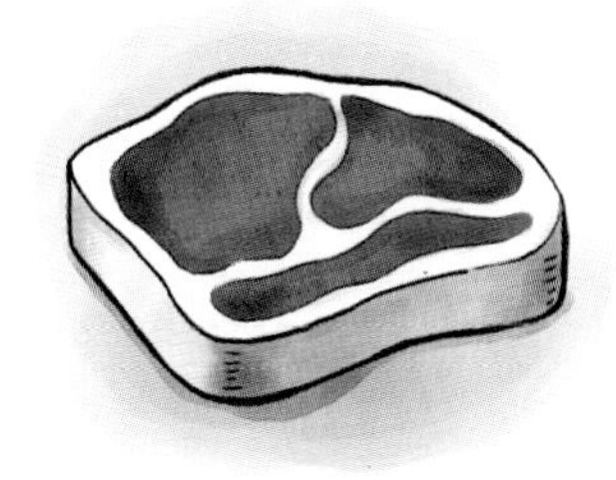

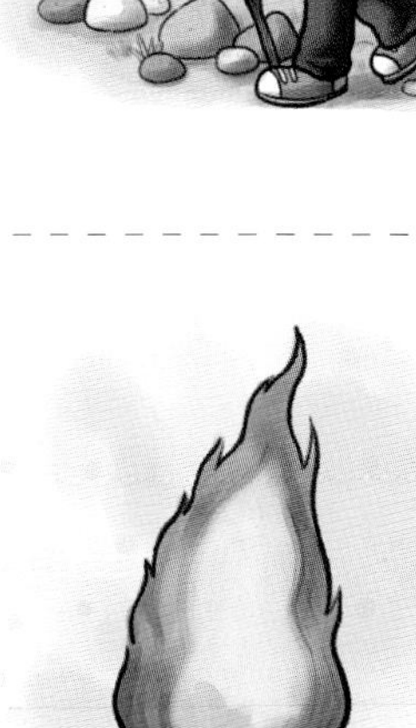

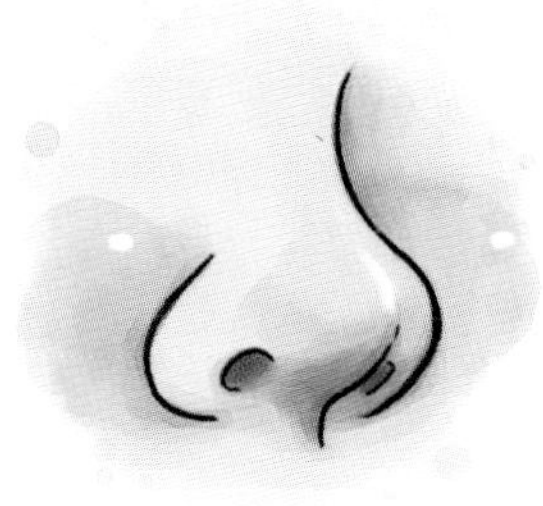

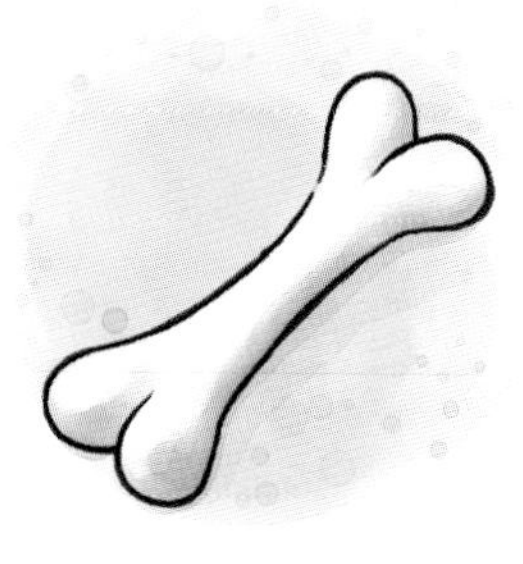

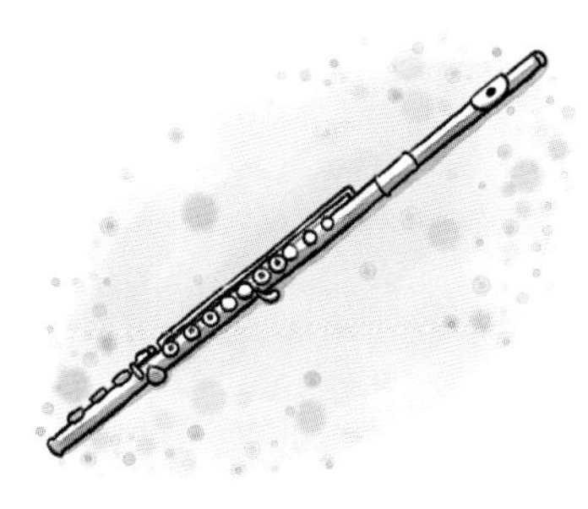

JUNE
SUN MON TUE WED THU FRI SAT

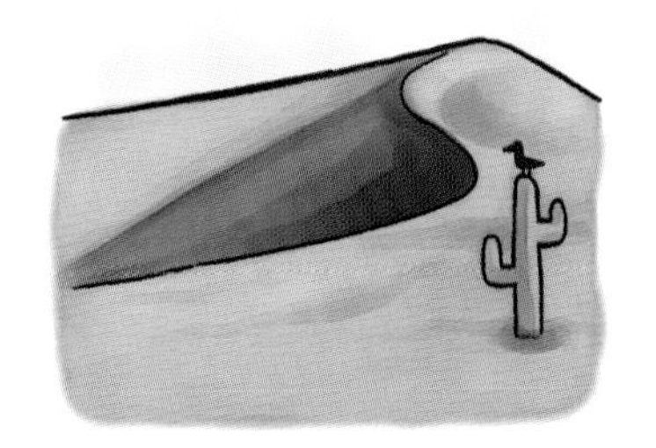

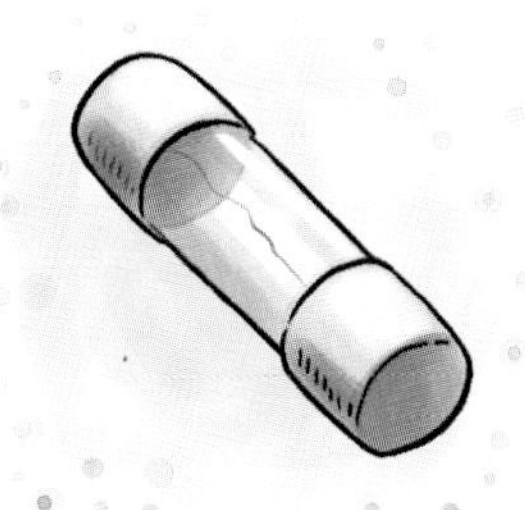

12
1
2
3
4
5
6
7
8
9
10
11

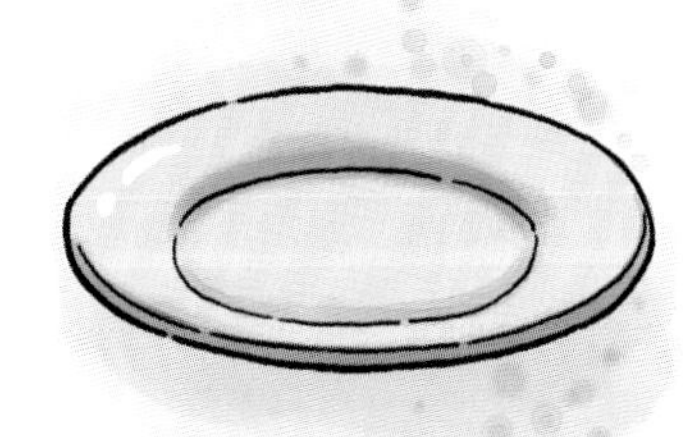

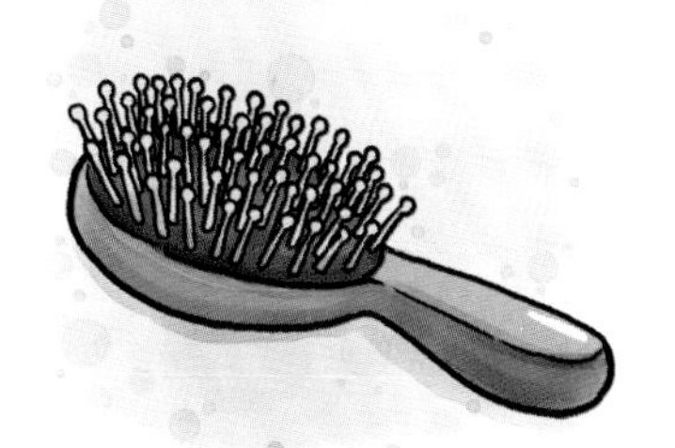

₩20,000

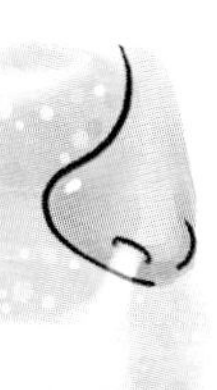

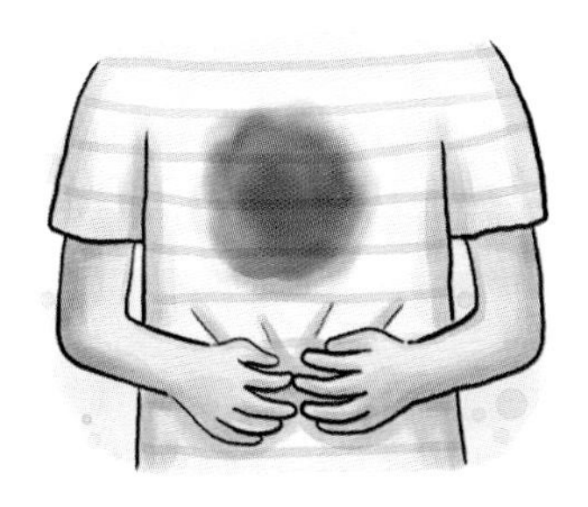

STOP

STORE

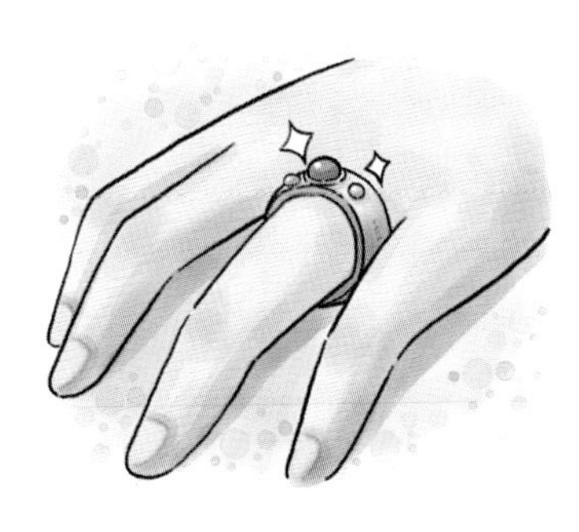

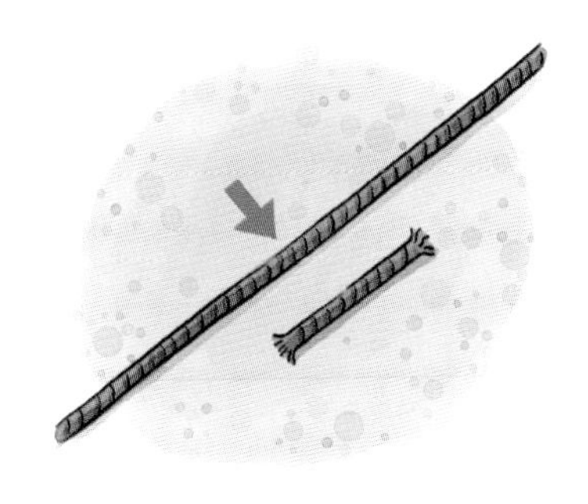

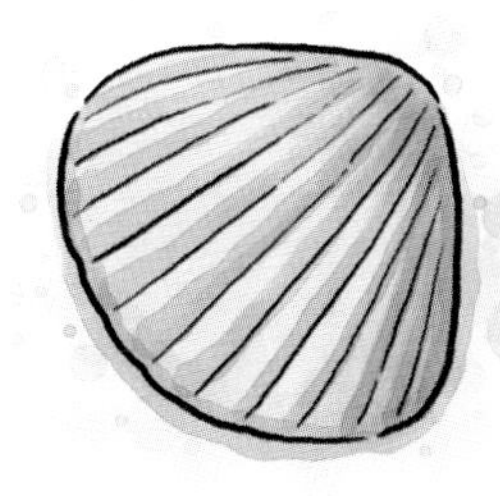

13

SOAP
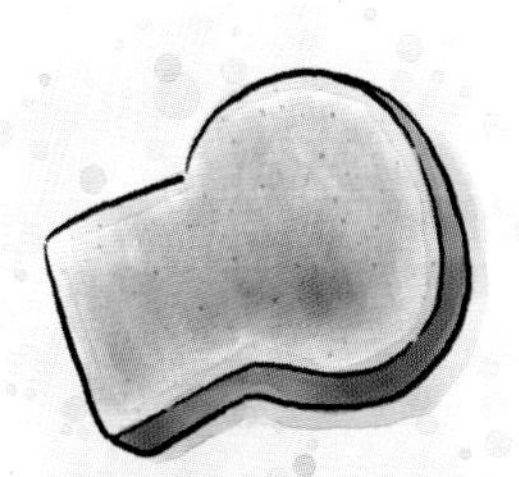

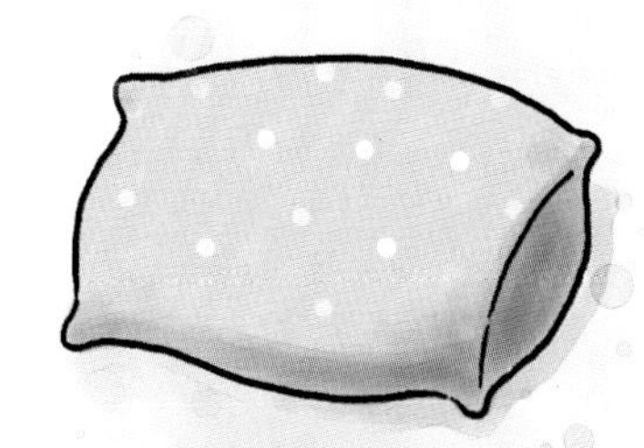

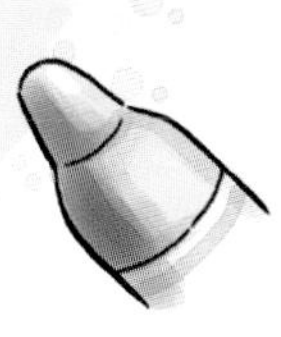

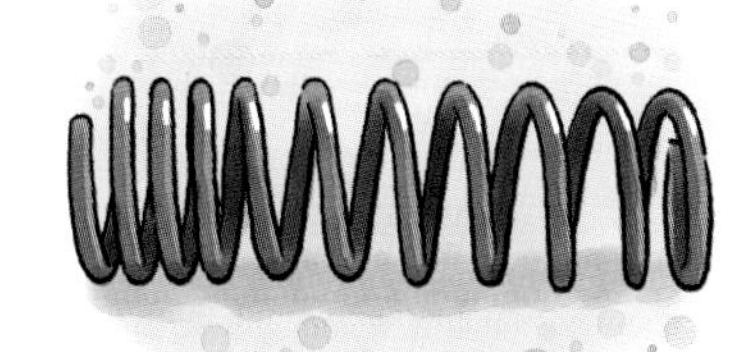

100

From:
To:

ENGLISH

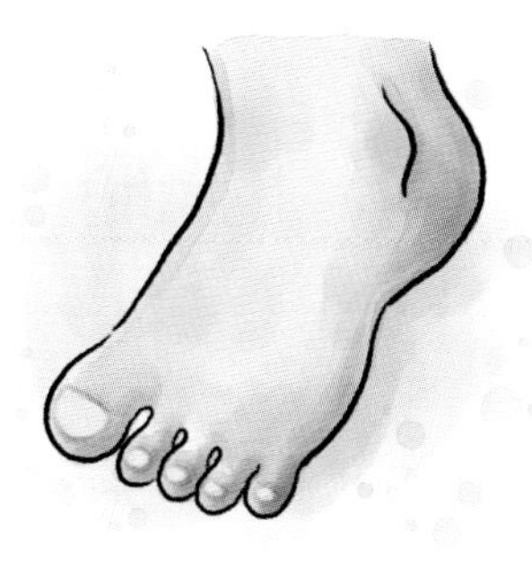

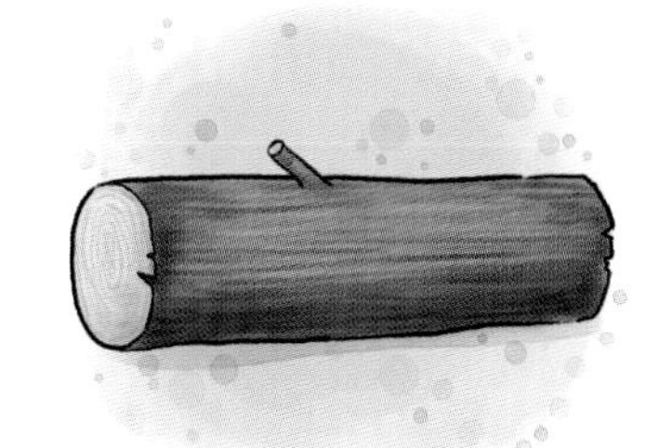

ZOO

Dog

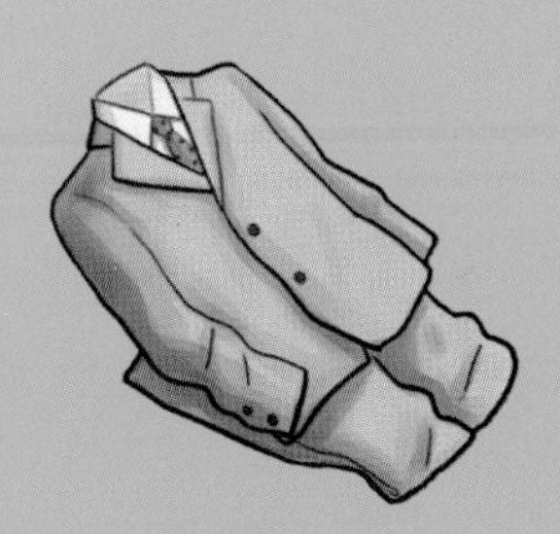

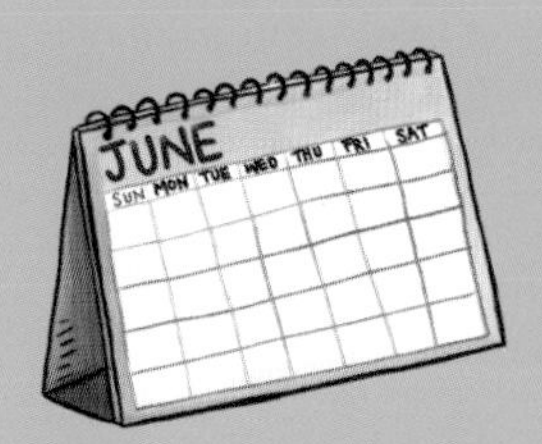

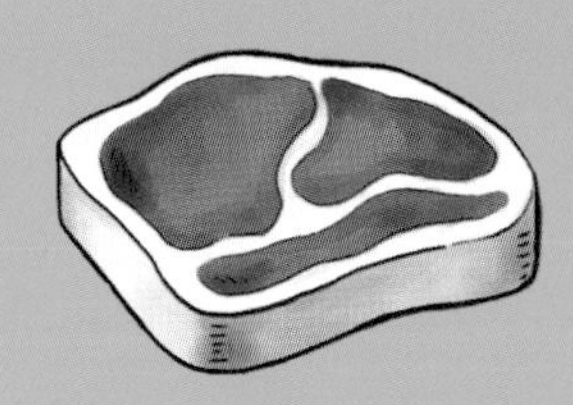

Put wings on your phonics!

Wing Wing Phonics 3

Workbook

Long Vowels &
Double Letter Sounds

Nexus Contents Development Team

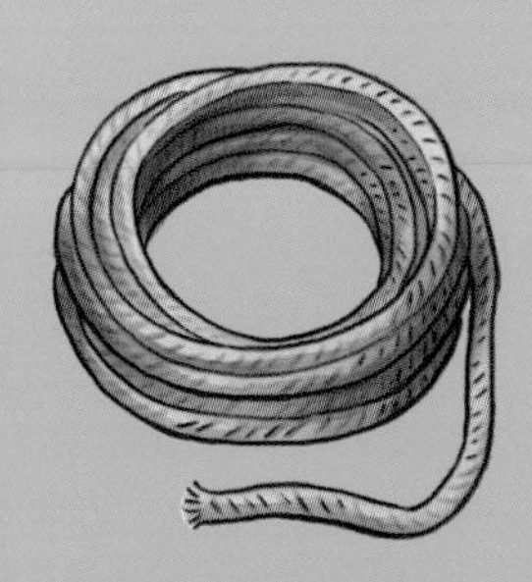

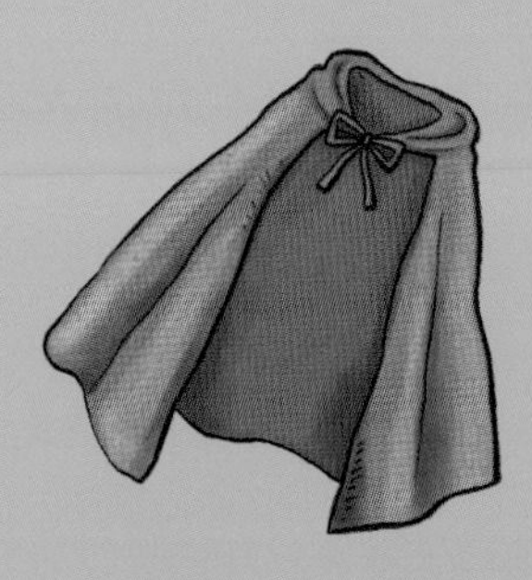

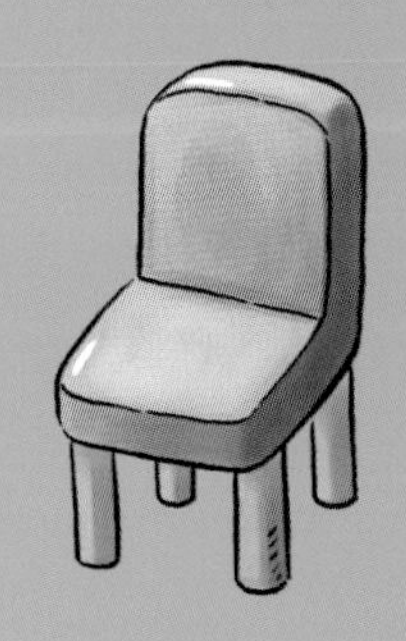

NEXUS Edu

Long Vowels &
Double Letter Sounds

Nexus Contents Development Team

Workbook

NEXUS Edu

 Finish the picture name.

 l ______

 c ______

-ape

 t ______

 c ______

-ace

 l ______

 r ______

-ase / -ane

 v ______

 c ______

Choose the correct word and write it.

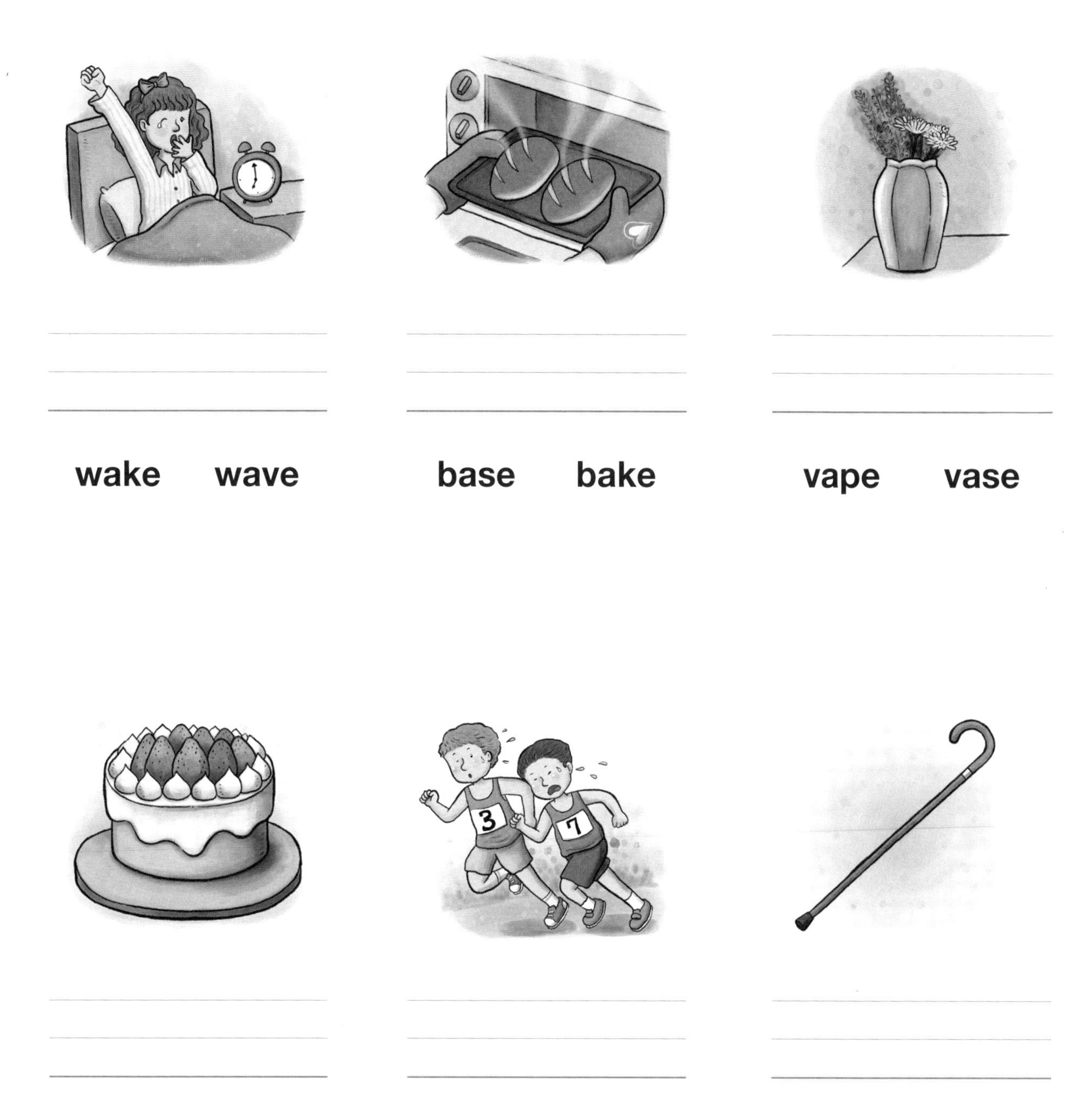

wake wave

base bake

vape vase

cake cale

race rake

cane case

Look at the picture and match the words.

cake lake bake wake cape

tape lace race cane vase

Write the correct word.

1. Mom ________s a ________ in the oven.
   bake lake　　lake cake

2. Emma wears a ________ with ________ .
   tape cape　　lace race

3. My grandmother with a ________ gets to the ________ .
   cane cape　　lake cake

 Choose the right picture.

tape   

vase   

lake   

 Cross out the word without long vowel /a/.

1.

wake

bee

vase

2.

peach

bake

lace

Unit 2 Long Vowel Ee

Finish the picture name.

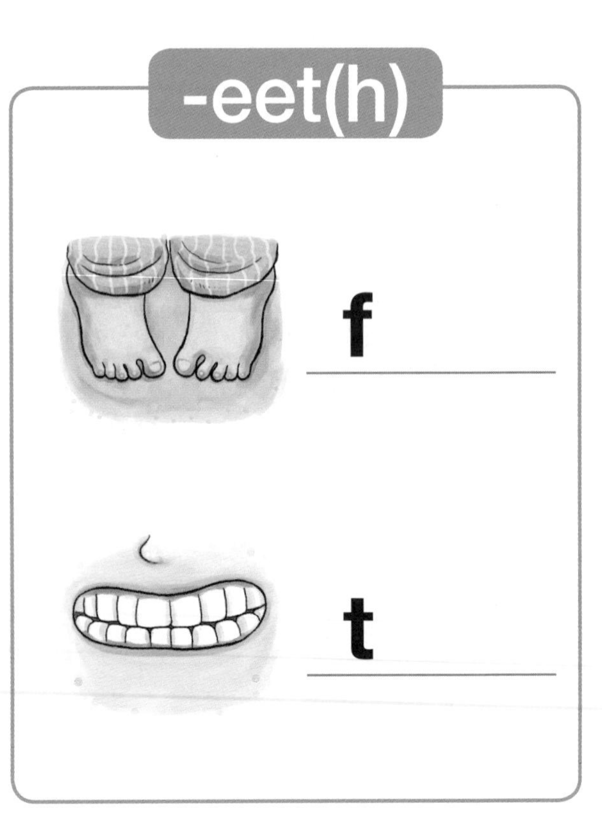

 Choose the correct word and write it.

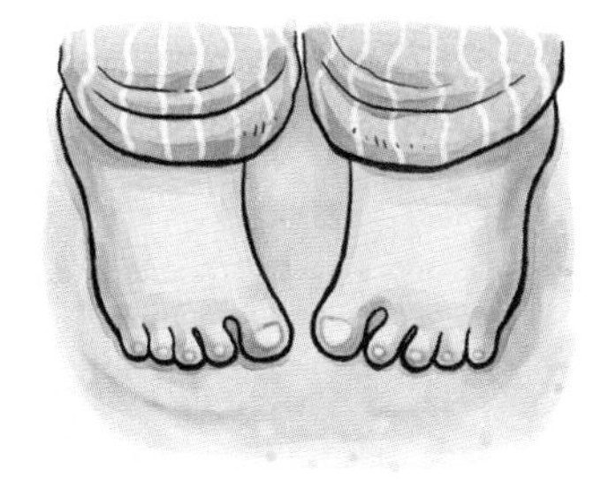

feet feat

tea tee

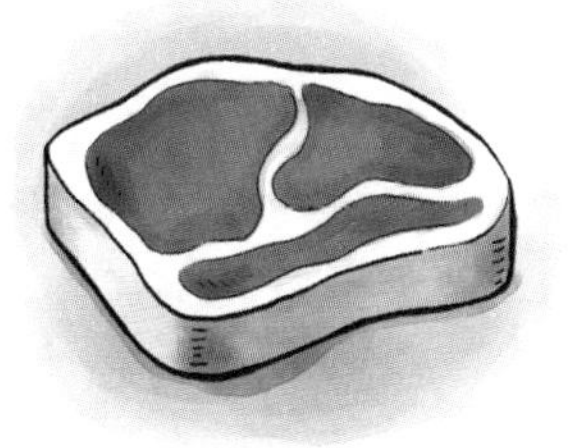

meet meat

bea bee

beech beach

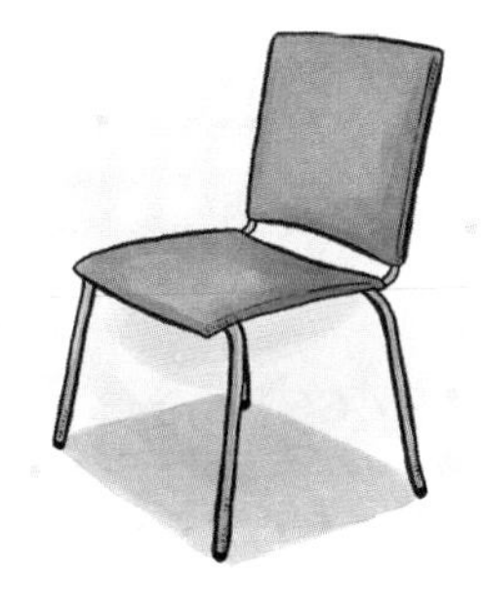

seat seet

Look at the picture and match the words.

bee tree feet teeth sea

tea beach peach meat seat

Write the correct word.

1. Willy sees a  ________ hive in a  ________.
   tree bee — tree bee

2. My family has 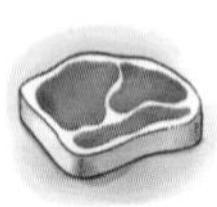 ________ and  ________es for lunch.
   meat seat — beach peach

3. Emma drinks orange juice on a  ________ by the  ________.
   beach peach — tea sea

 Choose the right picture.

teeth 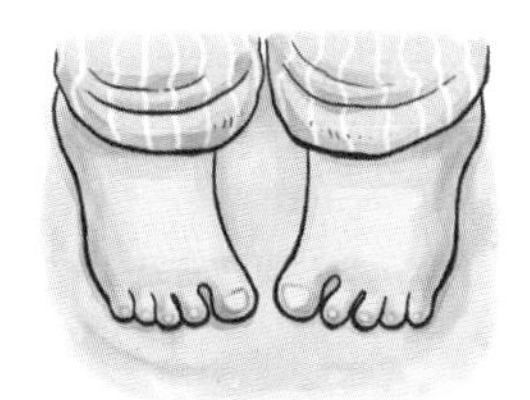  

seat  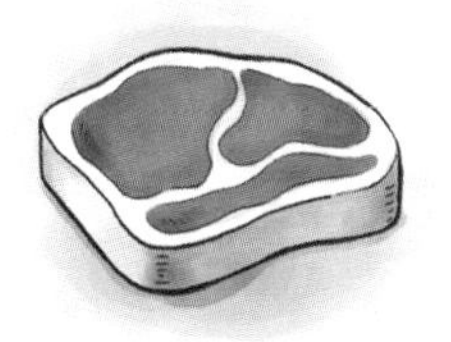 

tea  

 Cross out the word without long vowel /e/.

1.

 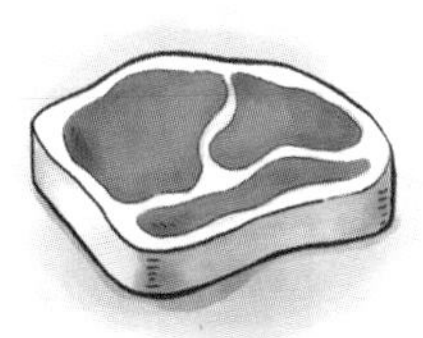 

tree **meat** **lake**

2.

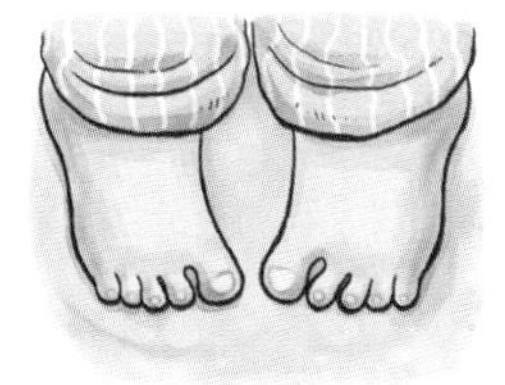 

feet **race** **beach**

Unit 3 Long Vowel Ii

Finish the picture name.

-ike

b ____________

h ____________

-ipe / -ire

p ____________

f ____________

-ite

b ____________

k ____________

-ive

f ____________

d ____________

 Choose the correct word and write it.

tire tare

wepe wipe

bite bate

kite kete

dive deve

pipe pepe

Look at the picture and match the words.

bike hike bite kite fire

tire dive five pipe wipe

Write the correct word.

1. Willy  ________s 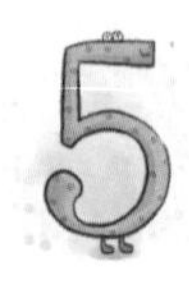 ________ times a day.
   dive five   five tire

2. Do not  ________ the  ________ .
   bike bite   fire tire

3. Emma with a  ________ gets off her  ________ .
   kite bite   bike hike

 Choose the right picture.

fire

wipe

pipe

 Cross out the word without long vowel /i/.

1.

sea **kite** **dive**

2.

five **tea** **bike**

 Finish the picture name.

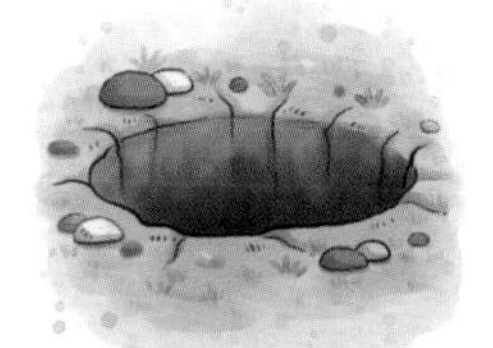 h ________

 m ________

-ome /-one

 h ________

 b ________

-ope

 h ________

 r ________

-ose

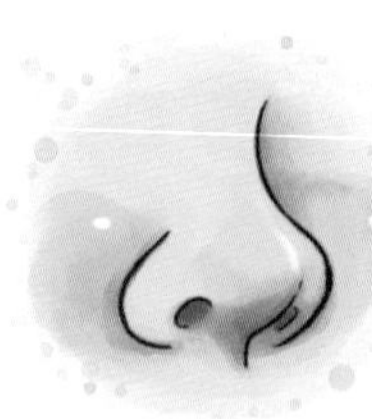 n ________

 r ________

 Choose the correct word and write it.

dome dame

home hame

rose rase

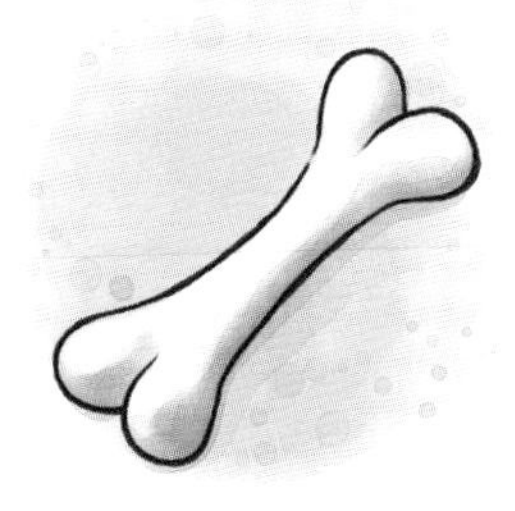

bone bane

nose nase

cone cane

Look at the picture and match the words.

hole mole hope rope nose

rose dome home bone cone

Write the correct word.

1. What a beautiful  ________ and a  ________ garden!

   home dome — nose rose

2. There is a big 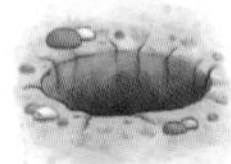 ________ near the ________ in the backyard.

   mole hole — bone cone

3. A  ________ jumps a 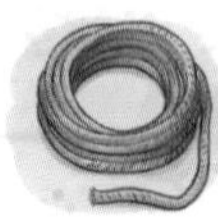 ________ .

   mole hole — rope hope

 Choose the right picture.

cone   

nose  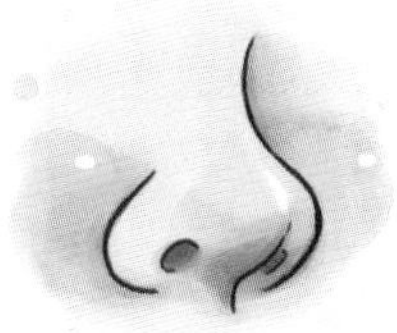 

hope   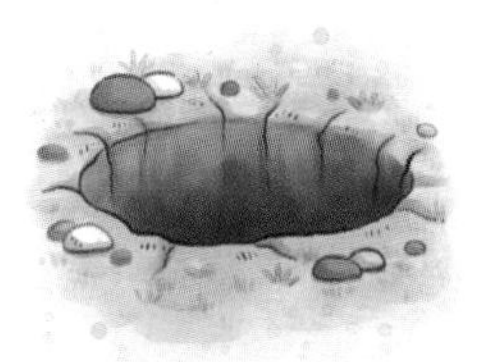

Cross out the word without long vowel /o/.

1.

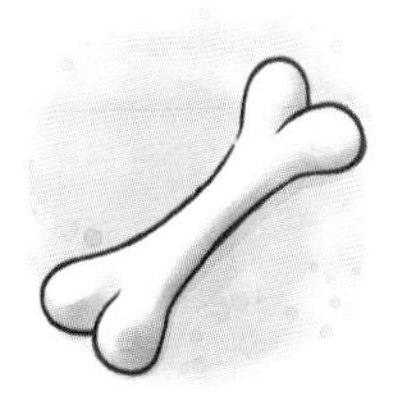  

bone **wipe** **mole**

2.

hike **rope** **dome**

Finish the picture name.

-ube

c ______

t ______

-uice / -uit

j ______

fr ______

-ule / -une

m ______

J ______

-use / -ute

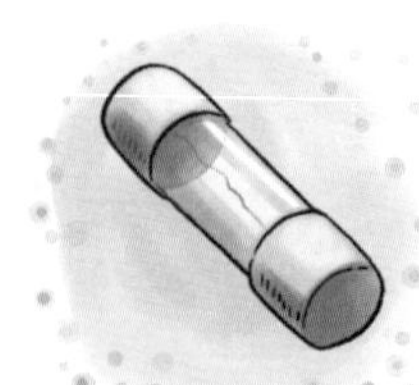

f ______

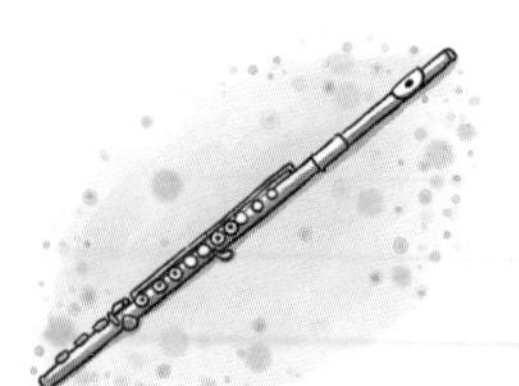

fl ______

Choose the correct word and write it.

dune dule

cabe cube

suit sate

tube tabe

June Jane

frate fruit

Look at the picture and match the words.

cube tube dune June flute

fuse mule juice fruit suit

Write the correct word.

1. Put ice ________s in the orange  ________ .

   tube cube — juice fruit

2. Emma starts playing the  ________ on  ________ 1st .

   fuse flute — dune June

3. Willy in a black 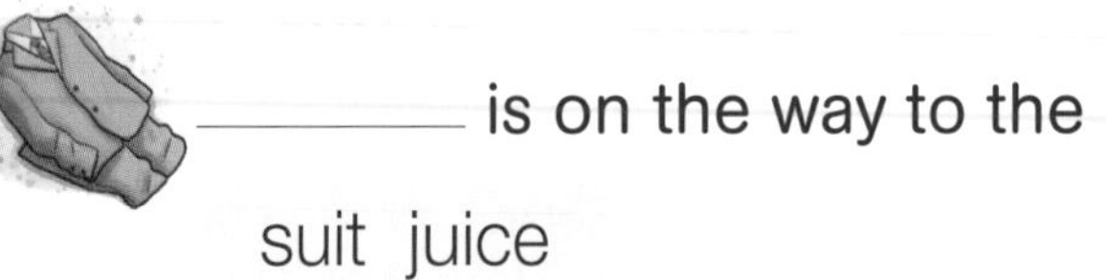 ________ is on the way to the  ________ shop.

   suit juice — fruit flute

Choose the right picture.

fuse

mule

tube

Cross out the word without long vowel /u/.

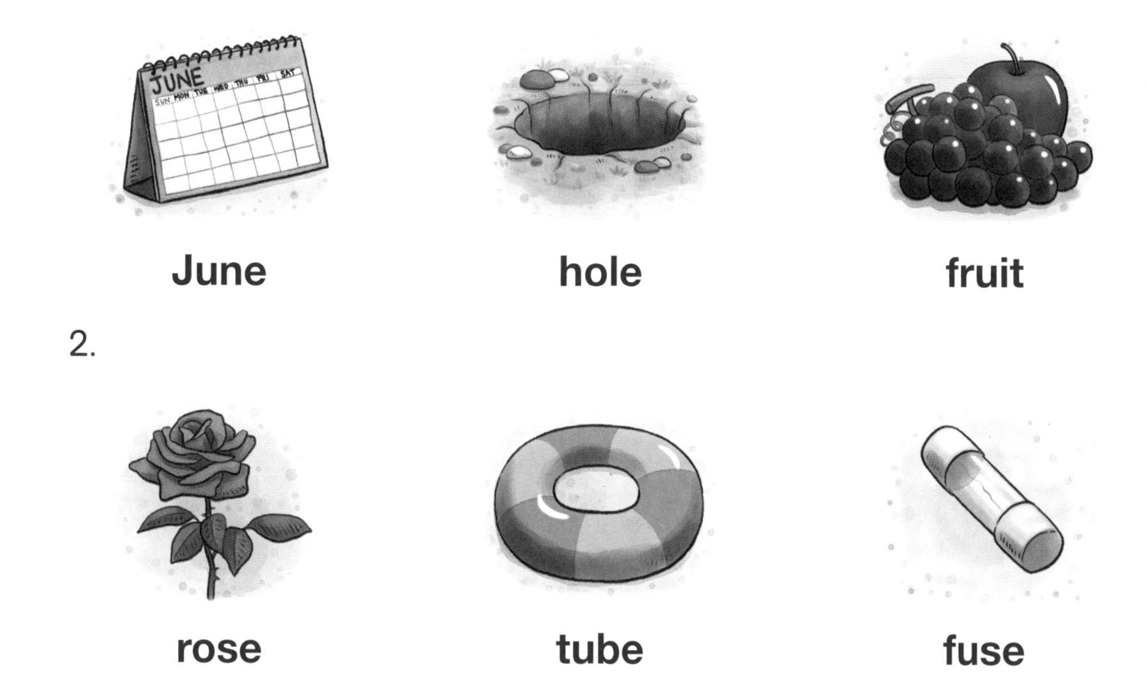

1.

June **hole** **fruit**

2.

rose **tube** **fuse**

Finish the picture name.

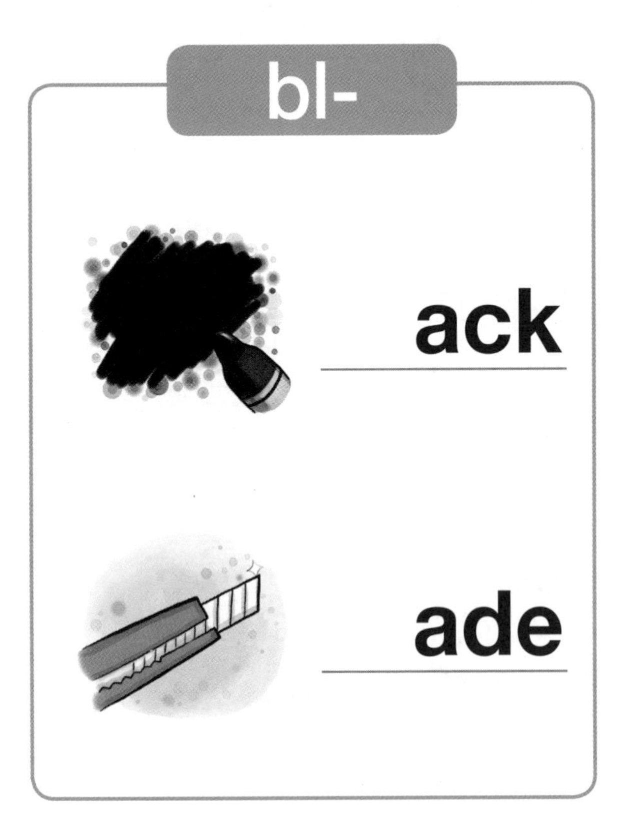

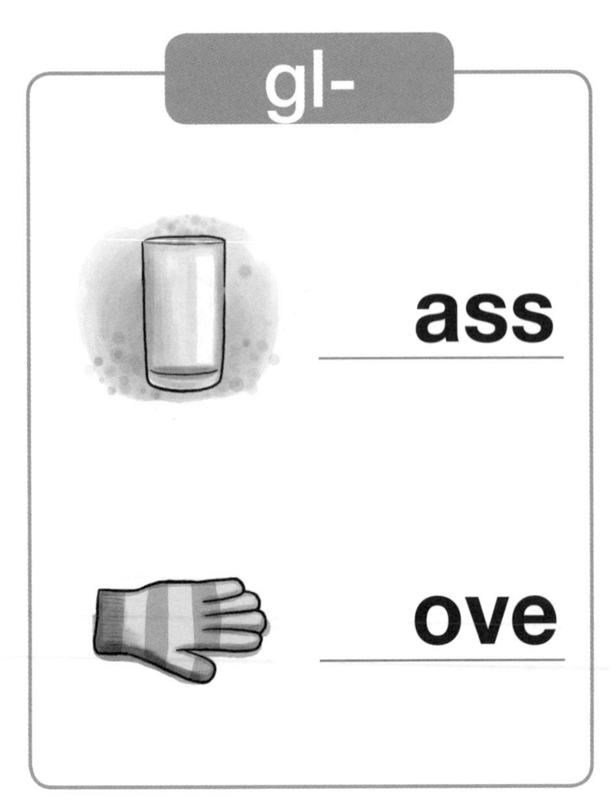

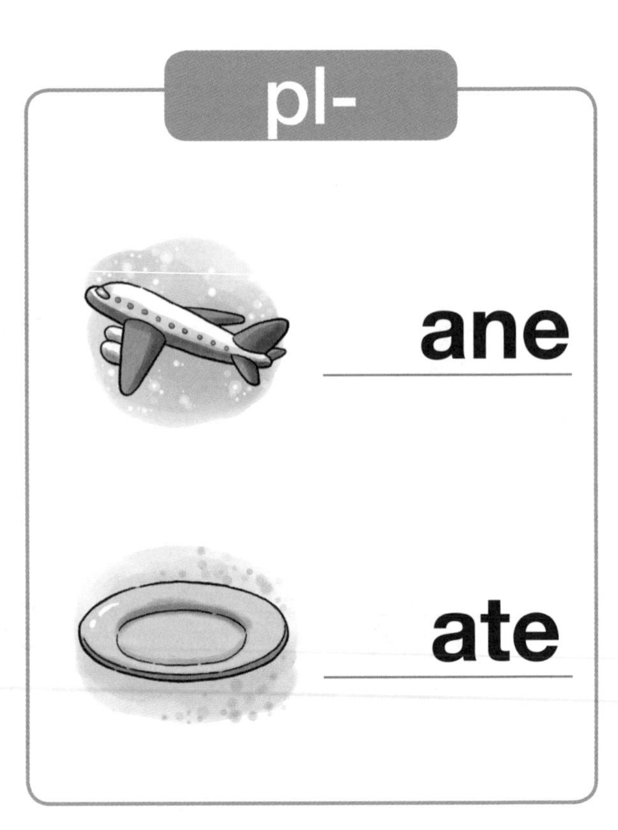

Choose the correct word and write it.

plant **blant**

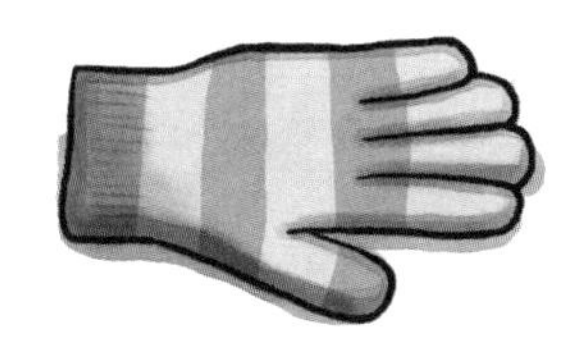

glove **clove**

clock **block**

blum **plum**

plane **blane**

plade **blade**

Look at the picture and match the words.

black blade classroom clock glass

glove plane plate plant plum

Write the correct word.

1. There is a  ________ on the 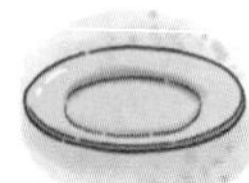 ________ !

   glass classroom — plate plant

2. Willy gets a  ________ model  ________ .

   black blade — plane plum

3. Look at the 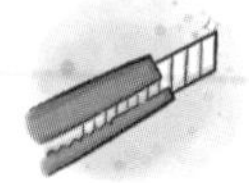 ________ and the  ________s on Willy's desk.

   black blade — glove clock

 Choose the right picture.

plant   

classroom   

plum 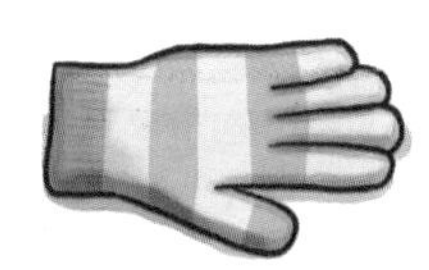 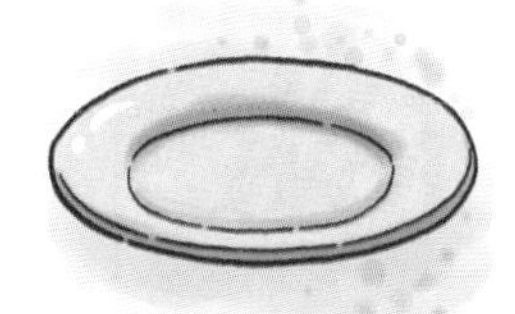 

 Cross out the word without l-blend /bl/, /cl/, /gl/ and /pl/.

1.

suit

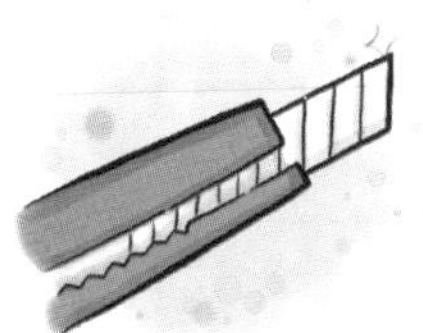
blade

plant

2.

black

dune

classroom

R-blend
br, dr, pr, tr

Finish the picture name.

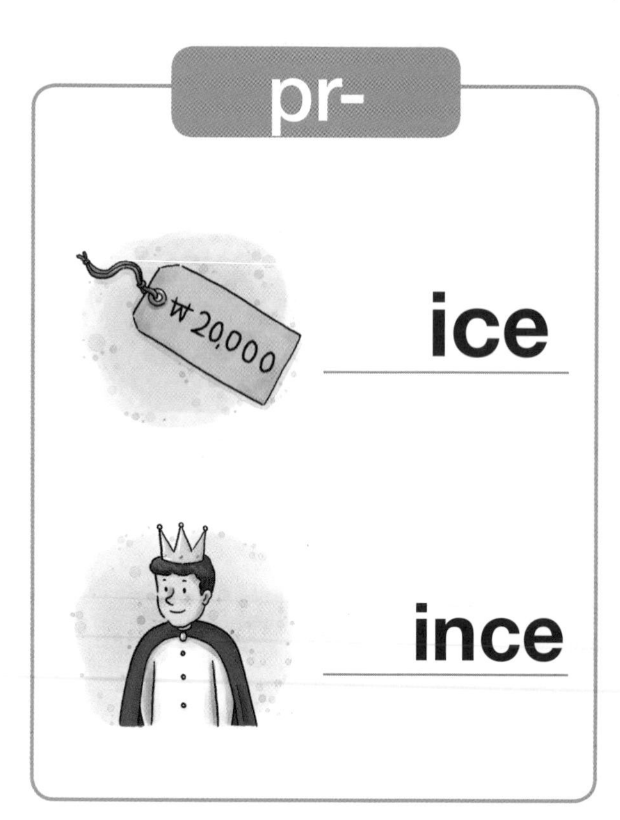

Choose the correct word and write it.

brush **drush**

press **dress**

tride **bride**

bread **dread**

bruck **truck**

drice **price**

 Look at the picture and match the words.

bread brush brick bride dress

drum price prince train truck

 Write the correct word.

1. Emma in a pink  ________ has  ________ .

   drum dress / bread brush

2. Look out for the  ________s in front of the  ________ .

   brick bride / drum dress

3. The  ________ gets on a  ________ at Seoul station.

   price prince / truck train

 Choose the right picture.

dress   

truck   

brush   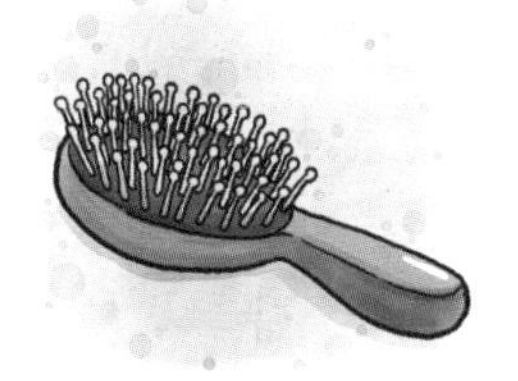

 Cross out the word without r-blend /br/, /dr/, /pr/ and /tr/.

1.

plum

price

prince

2.

drum

glove

train

 Finish the picture name.

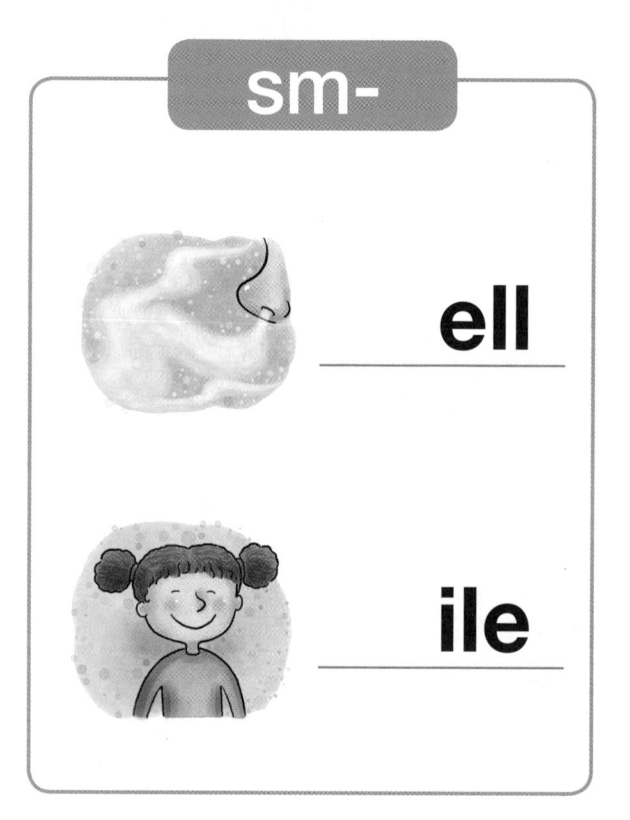

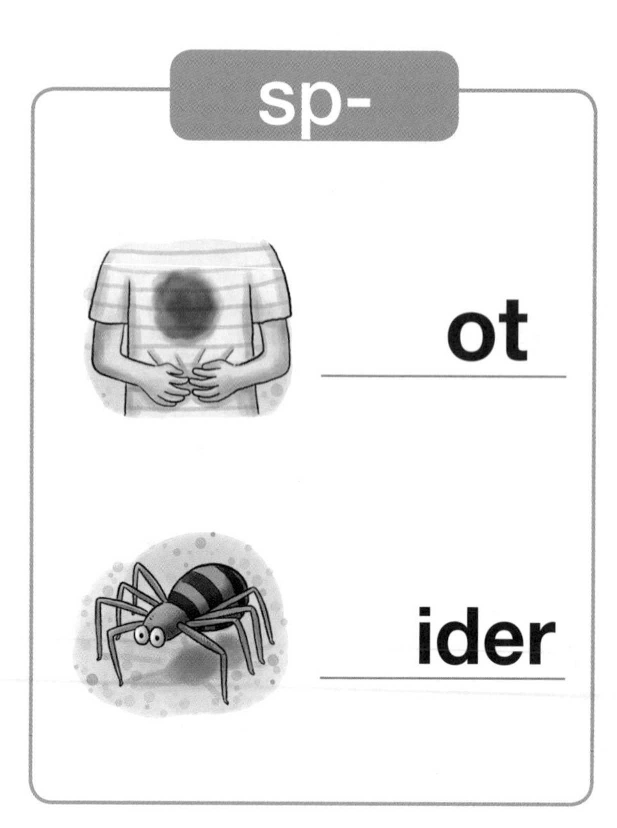

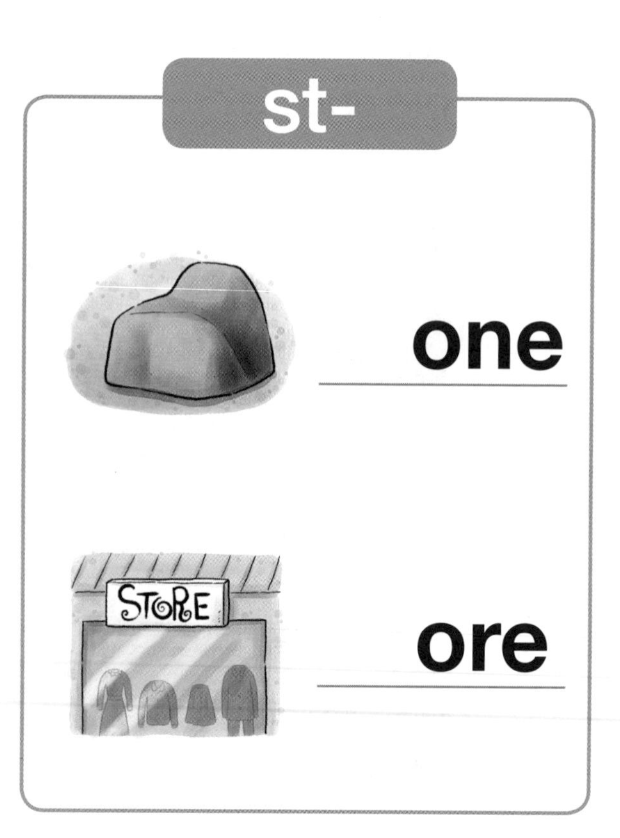

 Choose the correct word and write it.

smile snile

spore store

spider stider

spove stove

snop stop

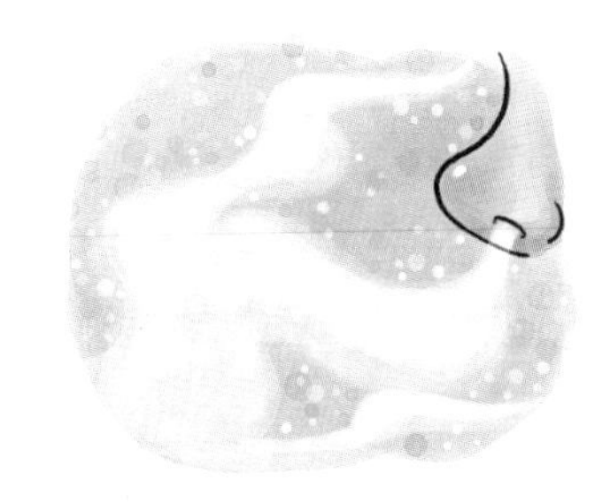

snell smell

Look at the picture and match the words.

smell smile snail snake spider

spot stone stop store stove

Write the correct word.

1. Emma with a  __________ (snail snake)  __________s happily. (smile smell)

2. A yam on the  __________ (store stove) __________s tasty. (smile smell)

3. A __________ (snail snake) is making  __________s on my jacket. (spot stop)

 Choose the right picture.

store

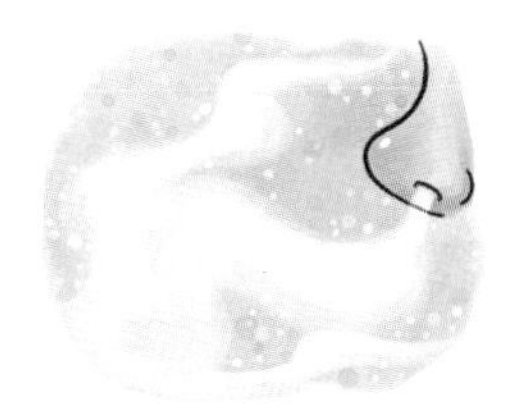

stop

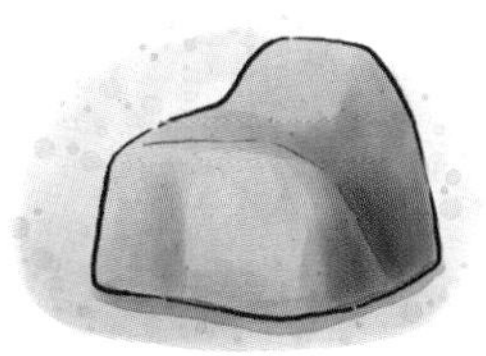

spider

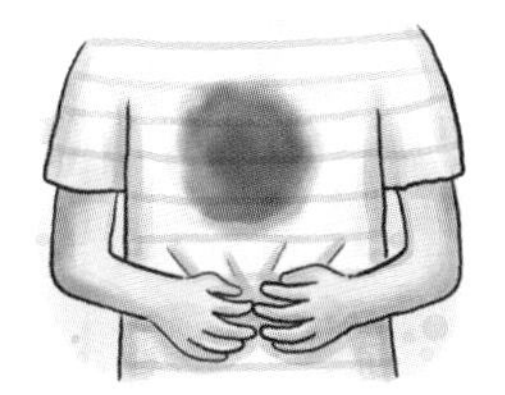

Cross out the word without s-blend /sm/, /sn/, /sp/ and /st/.

1.

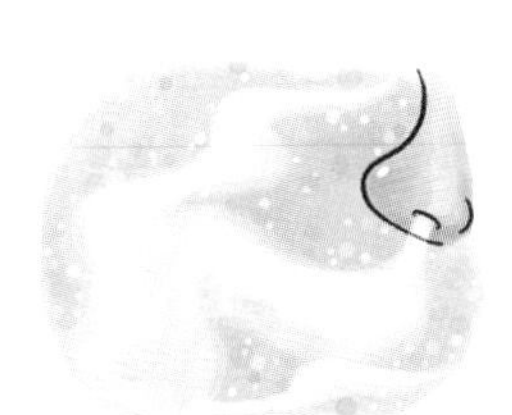

smell

bread

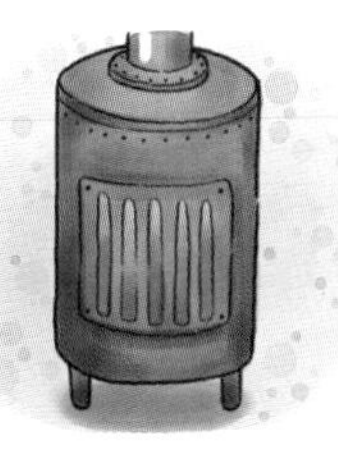

stove

2.

stone

snail

price

Unit 9 Ending-blend nd, ng, nk, nt

 Finish the picture name.

-nd

la ______

po ______

-ng

si ______

ri ______

-nk

wi ______

dri ______

-nt

a ______

te ______

Choose the correct word and write it.

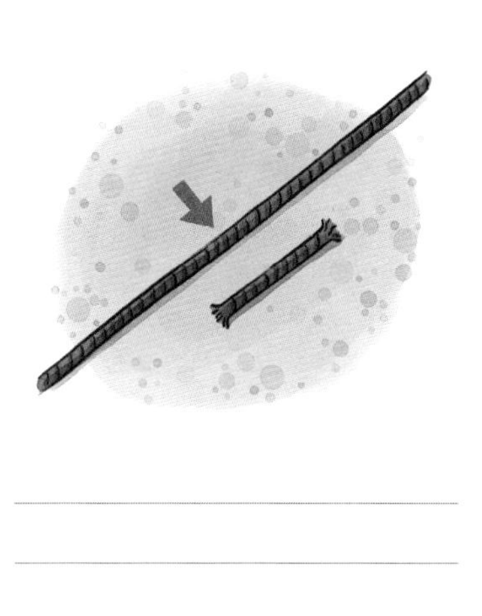

lond long

drind drink

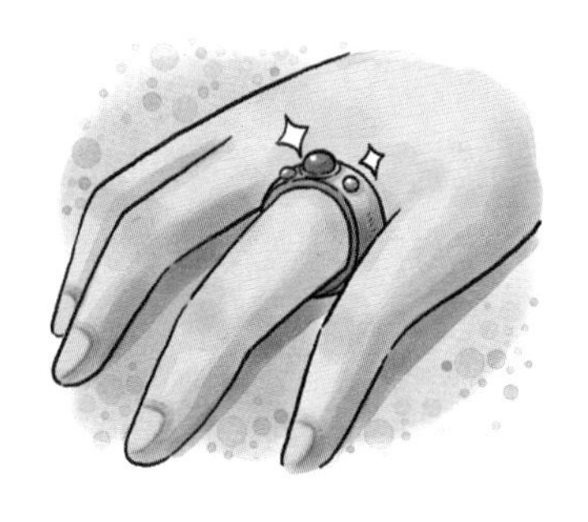

ring rink

pond pont

sink sing

wing wind

Look at the picture and match the words.

land pond sing wing long

ring drink wink ant tent

Write the correct word.

1. An ________ falls into a ________ .
   ant tent — land pond

2. The girl with ________ hair has a beautiful ________ .
   long ring — long ring

3. The parrot spreads its ________s and ________s on the nest.
   sing wing — sing wing

 Choose the right picture.

wink   

land  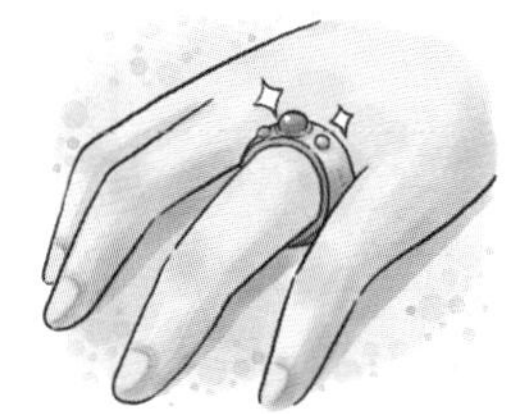 

tent   

 Cross out the word without ending-blend /nd/, /ng/, /nk/ and /nt/.

1.

sing **drink** **smile**

2.

 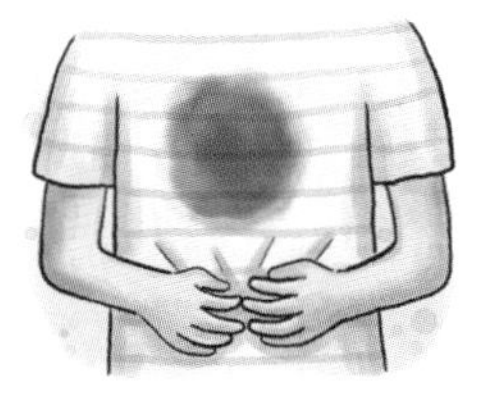 

ant **spot** **pond**

Digraph ch, ph, sh, th, wh

Finish the picture name.

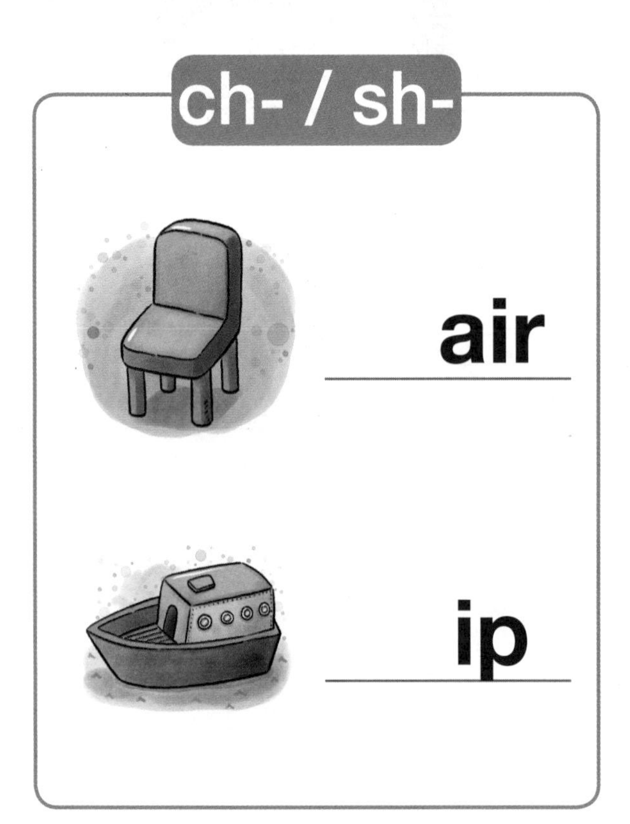

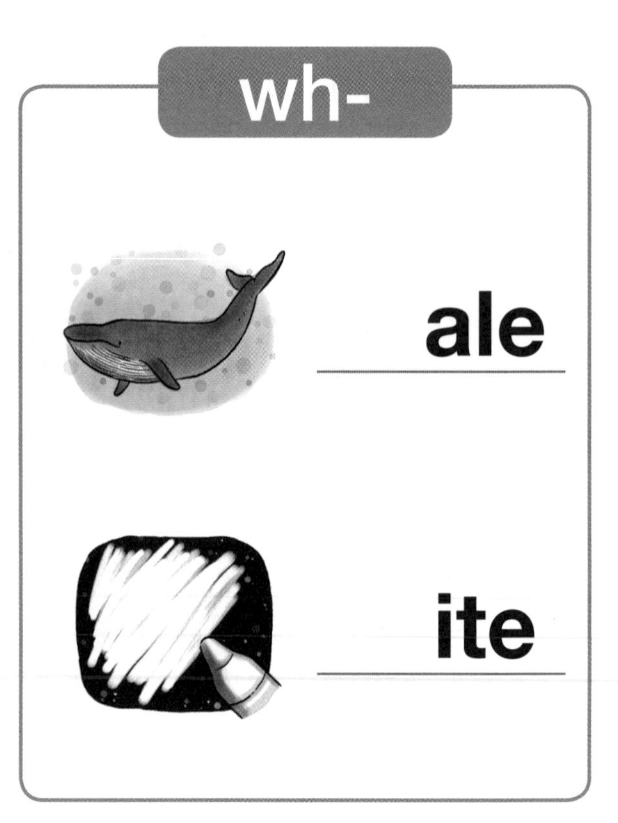

 Choose the correct word and write it.

pheese cheese

white chite

chell shell

phone thone

whair chair

choto photo

Look at the picture and match the words.

chair cheese phone photo shell

ship thirteen thumb whale white

Write the correct word.

1. Willy takes a  ________ with a toy  ________ .
   phone photo　　　whale white

2. A mouse on a  ________ eats  ________ .
   ship shell　　　chair cheese

3. Emma puts a  ________  ________ next to the window.
   whale white　　　cheese chair

 Choose the right picture.

thumb   

whale   

shell  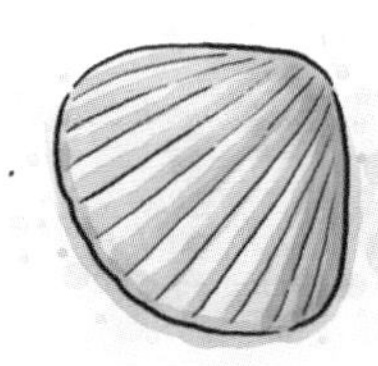 

 Cross out the word without digraph /ch/, /ph/, /sh/, /th/ and /wh/.

1.

ship **thirteen** **tent**

2.

pond **photo** **chair**

Double Letter Vowels
oa, ow

Finish the picture name.

-oa-

-ow

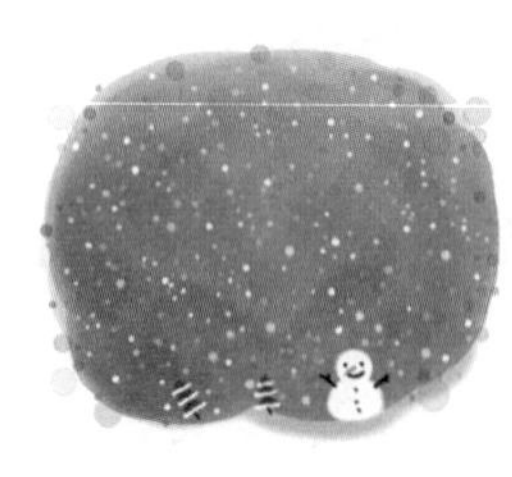

Choose the correct word and write it.

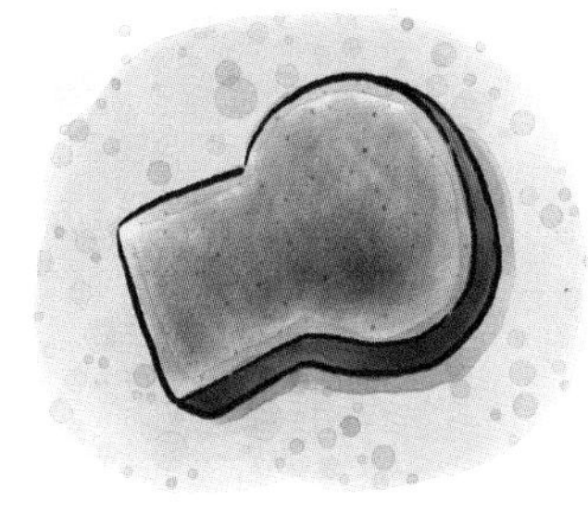

toast toust

bowl boast

cout coat

snow snaw

soap soup

pillaw pillow

 Look at the picture and match the words.

boat coat goat soap toast

bowl pillow snow window yellow

 Write the correct word.

1. The house has  ________  ________s.
   pillow yellow snow window

2. Willy in a rain  ________ plays in the 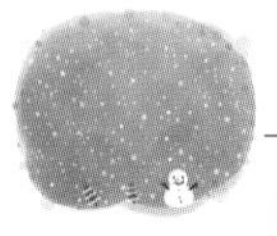 ________ .
   boat coat pillow snow

3. Mom cleans a  ________ with a dish 

________ .
   bowl pillow soap goat

Choose the right picture.

goat

pillow

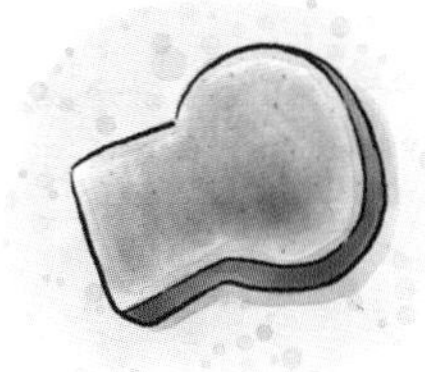

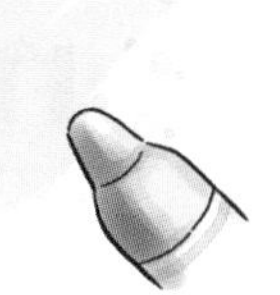

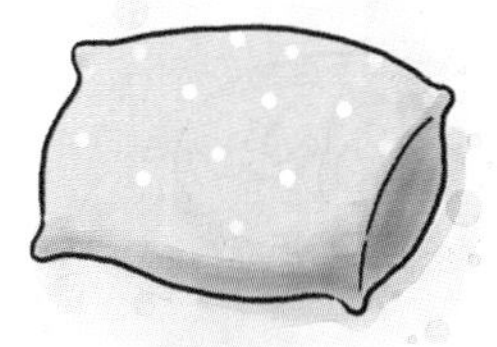

boat

Cross out the word without double letter vowels /oa/ and /ow/.

1.

bowl

shell

snow

2.

coat

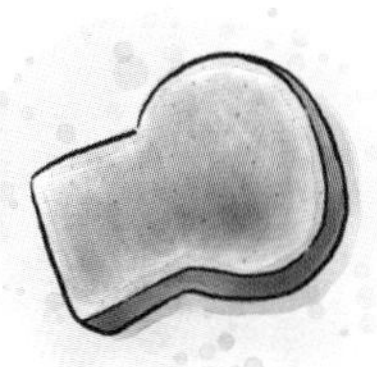

toast

thumb

Double Letter Vowels
oi, oy

Finish the picture name.

-oi-

c ___ n

p ___ nt

s ___ l

t ___ let

-oy(-)

b ______

t ______

j ______

______ ster

Choose the correct word and write it.

coal coil

boy bog

coin coan

toolet toilet

tos toy

boil bowl

Look at the picture and match the words.

boil soil coil coin point

toilet boy joy toy oyster

Write the correct word.

1. Emma ________s to an ________ at a fish market.
   point toilet — toy oyster

2. A ________ is in front of the ________.
   joy boy — toilet coil

3. Look at the ________ in the ________.
   coil coin — soil boil

Choose the right picture.

boil

toilet

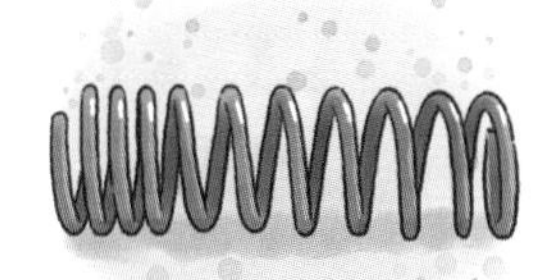

joy

Cross out the word without double letter vowels /oi/ and /oy/.

1.

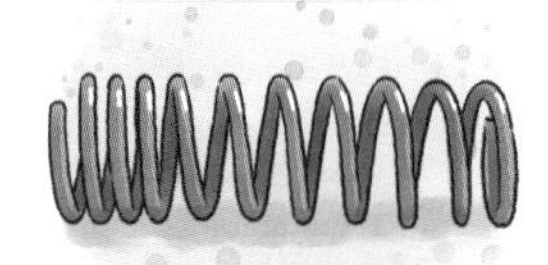

coat **coil** **coin**

2.

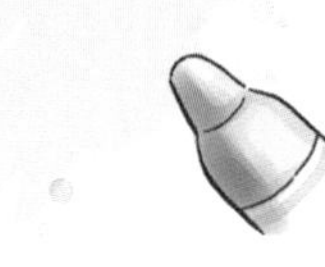

boy **yellow** **oyster**

Double Letter Vowels
ou, ow

Finish the picture name.

-ou-

l ___ d

h ___ se

cl ___ d

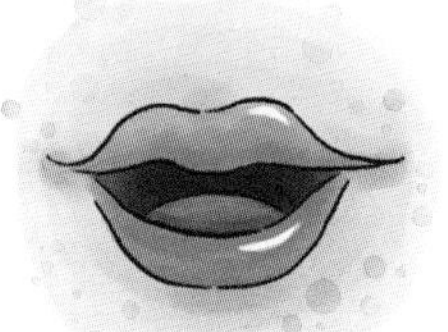

m ___ th

-ow-

c ___

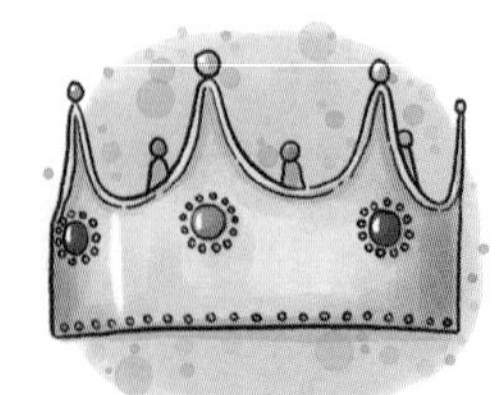

cr ___ n

br ___ n

cl ___ n

Choose the correct word and write it.

house hose

brown broun

cloud clod

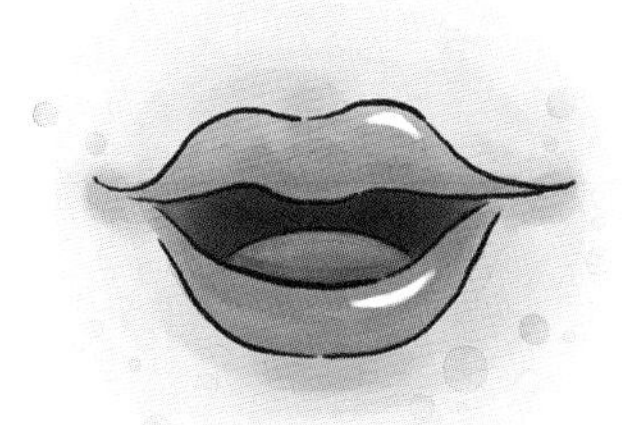

mouth month

goun gown

owl oil

Look at the picture and match the words.

cloud loud house mouth cow

owl gown crown brown clown

Write the correct word.

1. Willy sees an  ________ in the  ________.
   owl cow — mouth house

2. Look at the  ________  ________ in the sky.
   brown clown — cloud loud

3. A  ________ has a  ________.
   cow owl — mouth house

Choose the right picture.

crown

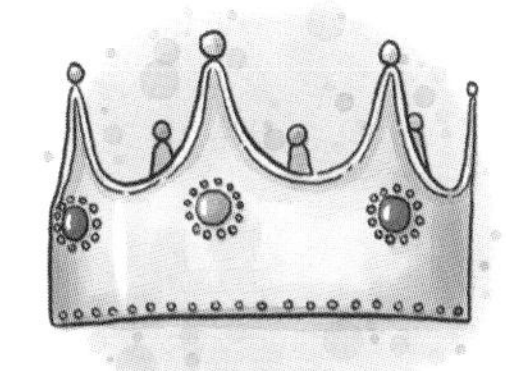  

loud

clown

Cross out the word without double letter vowels /ou/ and /ow/.

1.

gown **house** **joy**

2.

mouth **brown** **boil**

Unit 14 Double Letter Vowels er, ir, ur

Finish the picture name.

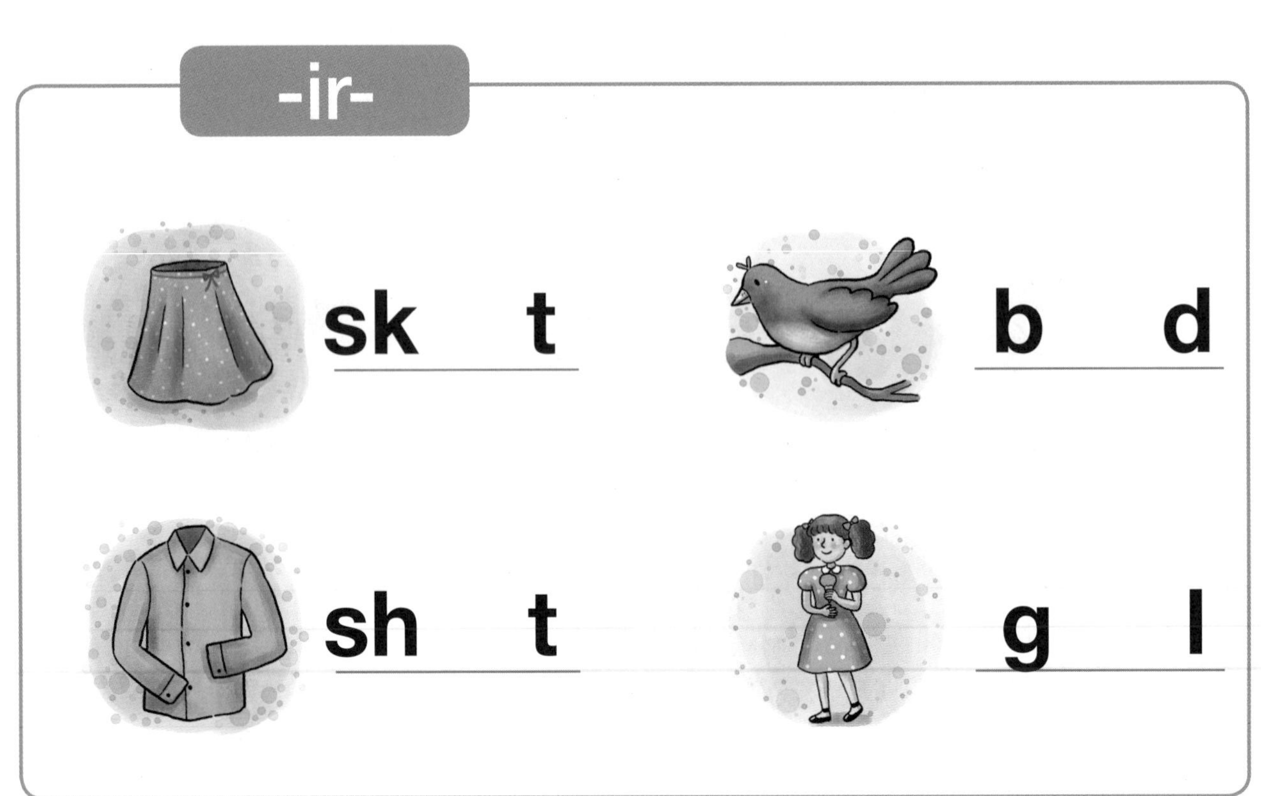

Choose the correct word and write it.

farmer farmur

girl gerl

nirse nurse

singur singer

perse purse

berd bird

Look at the picture and match the words.

letter singer farmer teacher bird

girl shirt skirt nurse purse

Write the correct word.

1. My ________ sent me a ________ .
   nurse teacher — letter singer

2. A ________ feeds bread to the ________s.
   farmer singer — girl bird

3. The ________ likes to wear a ________ .
   farmer singer — skirt shirt

 Choose the right picture.

purse   

skirt 

singer   

 Cross out the word without double letter vowels /er/, /ir/ and /ur/.

1.

shirt **cow** **bird**

2.

farmer **nurse** **cloud**

Double Letter Vowels

oo

Finish the picture name.

-oo-

b ___ k

f ___ d

c ___ k

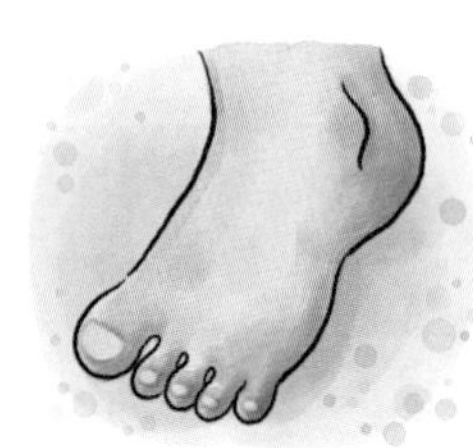

f ___ t

m ___ n

g ___ se

sp ___ n

z ___

 Choose the correct word and write it.

pool peel

goase goose

zoo zee

weed wood

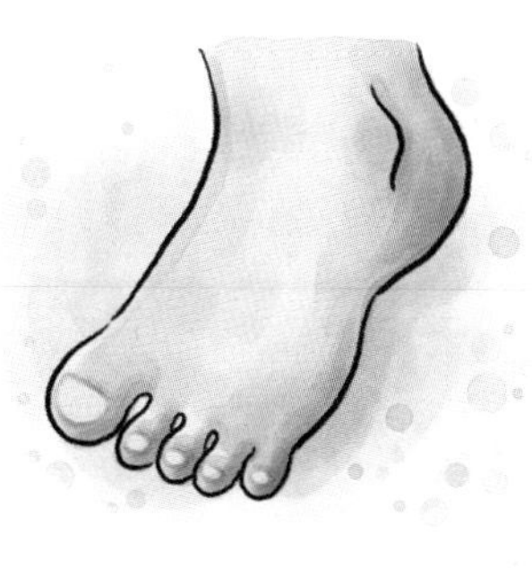

feat foot

cook coak

Look at the picture and match the words.

book cook food foot goose

moon pool spoon wood zoo

Write the correct word.

1. Mom ________s ________.
   cook book / foot food

2. A ________ swims in the ________.
   goose moon / spoon pool

3. Willy lost his ________ in a ________.
   book cook / wood zoo

Choose the right picture.

foot

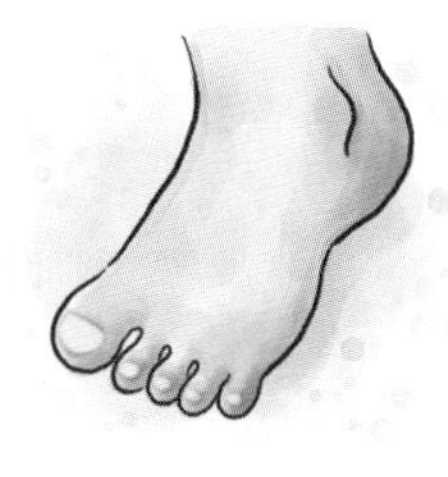

wood

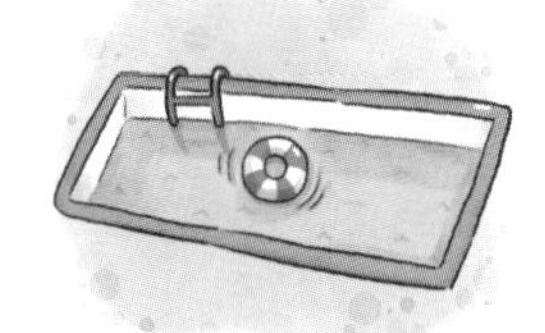

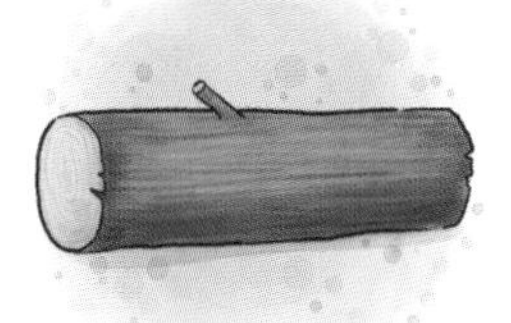

moon

Cross out the word without double letter vowels /oo/.

1.

pool

singer

book

2.

nurse

spoon

cook

memo~

memo~

Wing Wing Phonics 3

Wing Wing Phonics is a three-book phonics series designed for elementary school students. The main purpose of this phonics series is to develop basic English sounds through a systematic presentation of the alphabet, vowel combinations, and consonant blends. The series has charming, full-color illustrations and a variety of activities that will stimulate the learners' interest.

Features

- Activities to build listening skills
- Review units featuring fun games
- Chants and stories to review sounds, letters, and words
- A test included in the Teacher's Materials
- A colorful illustrated glossary of key vocabularies
- An accompanying individual workbook with writing activities

Components of the Series

- Wing Wing Phonics 1 Alphabet
- Wing Wing Phonics 2 Single Letter Sounds
- Wing Wing Phonics 3 Long Vowels & Double Letter Sounds

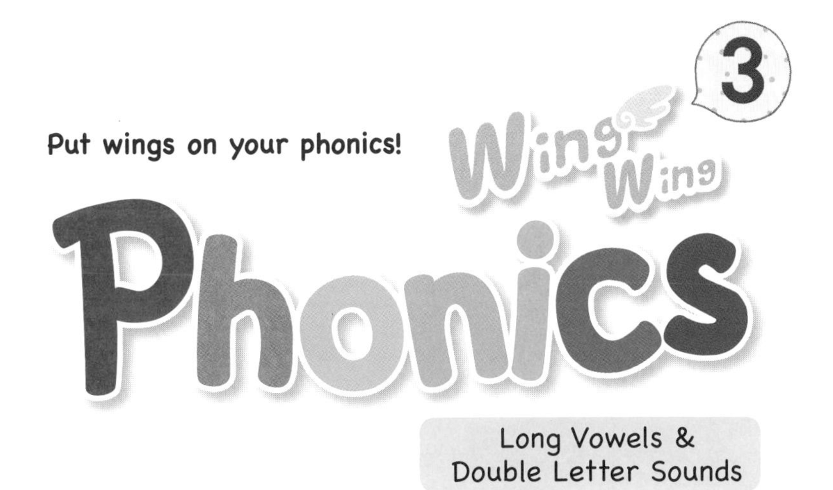

Answers

NEXUS Edu

Unit 1 Long Vowel Aa

Emma invites Willy to her house. She is baking a cake for him.

-a-e

cake lake bake wake cape

tape lace race cane vase

6

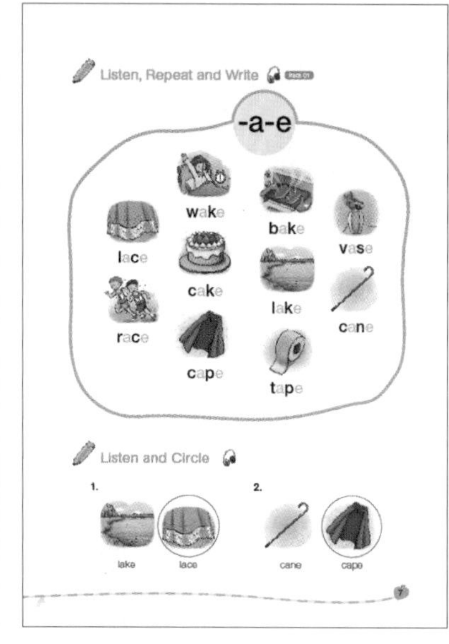

Listen, Repeat and Write

-a-e

wake bake lace vase cake lake race cane cape tape

Listen and Circle

1. lake lace
2. cane cape

7

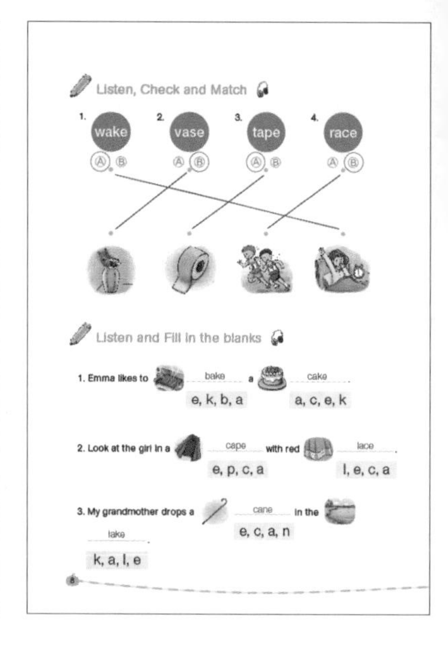

Listen, Check and Match

1. wake Ⓐ Ⓑ
2. vase Ⓐ Ⓑ
3. tape Ⓐ Ⓑ
4. race Ⓐ Ⓑ

Listen and Fill in the blanks

1. Emma likes to bake (e, k, b, a) a cake (a, c, e, k).
2. Look at the girl in a cape (e, p, c, a) with red lace (l, e, c, a).
3. My grandmother drops a cane (e, c, a, n) in the lake (k, a, l, e).

8

Listen, Read and Play

Today is Rabbit's birthday. Koko bakes a cake for Rabbit.
Koko goes to the lake. Rabbit is under the peach tree by the lake.

Koko: Happy Birthday, Rabbit! Here's a birthday cake for you!
Rabbit: Oh thanks, but I don't eat cakes.
Koko: Oh...then, what do you want?
Rabbit: Hmmm.... Your cape is pretty. I like the red lace.
It will look nice on my table under my flower vase.
Koko: Oh.... Uh...okay, you can have my cape with red lace.

Write the words with long /a/ sound in the story.

bake, cake, lake, cape, lace, vase

Good Job!!!

9

Unit 2 Long Vowel Ee

Emma's family has a picnic on the beach.

-ee-
-ea-

bee tree feet teeth sea

tea beach peach meat seat

10

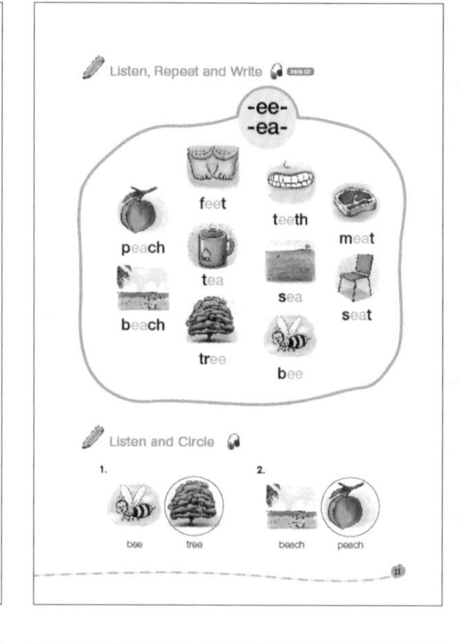

Listen, Repeat and Write

-ee-
-ea-

feet teeth peach meat tea sea beach seat tree bee

Listen and Circle

1. bee tree
2. beach peach

11

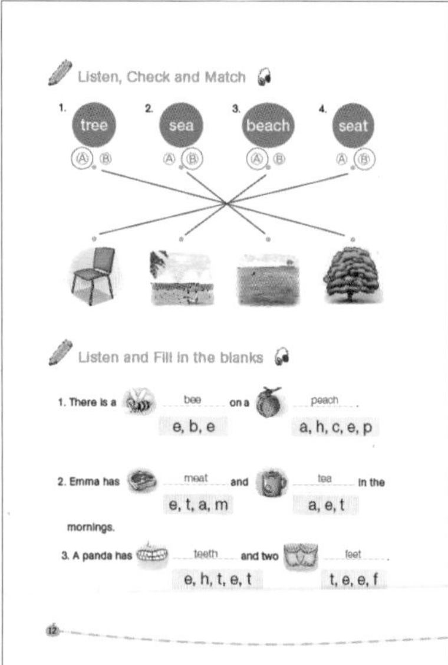

Listen, Check and Match

1. tree Ⓐ Ⓑ
2. sea Ⓐ Ⓑ
3. beach Ⓐ Ⓑ
4. seat Ⓐ Ⓑ

Listen and Fill in the blanks

1. There is a bee (e, b, e) on a peach (a, h, c, e, p).
2. Emma has meat (e, t, a, m) and tea (a, e, t) in the mornings.
3. A panda has teeth (e, h, t, e, t) and two feet (t, e, e, f).

12

Listen, Read and Play

It is a beautiful sunny day at the beach.
Koko and Bobo find two seats under a tree.
They sit and drink juice.

Bobo: Wow, there are many people in the sea!
Koko: Bobo, do you want to go swim in the sea?
Bobo: Nah...I ate a big lunch.
Koko: What did you eat?
Bobo: I had a peach, some meat and a bee with honey.
Koko: You ate a bee?!!
Bobo: Uh...It just flew into my mouth!

Write the words with long /e/ sound in the story.

beach, seat, tree, sea, peach, meat, bee

Good Job!!!

13

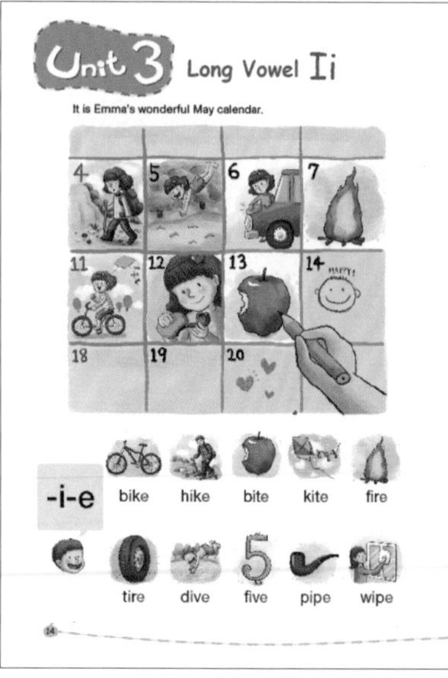

Unit 3 Long Vowel Ii

It is Emma's wonderful May calendar.

4 5 6 7 11 12 13 14 18 19 20

-i-e

bike hike bite kite fire

tire dive five pipe wipe

14

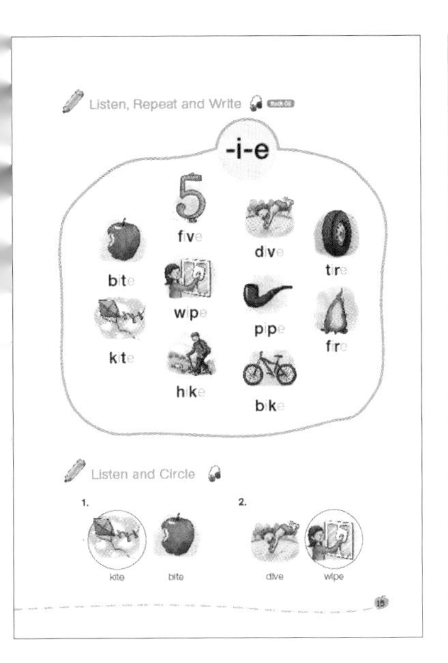

Listen, Repeat and Write

-i-e

five, dive, tire, bite, wipe, pipe, kite, fire, hike, bike

Listen and Circle

1. kite bite
2. dive wipe

15

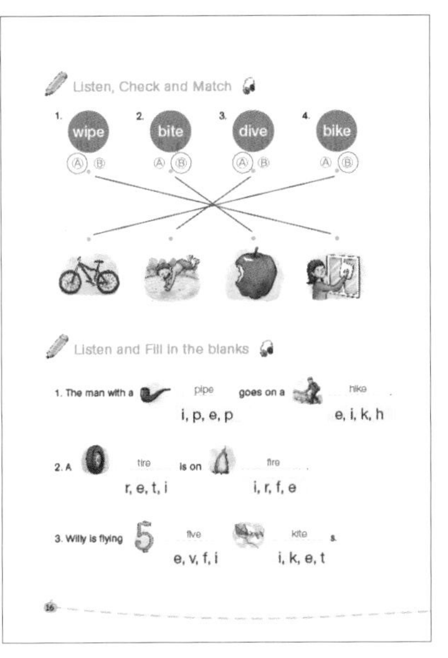

Listen, Check and Match

1. wipe Ⓐ Ⓑ
2. bite Ⓐ Ⓑ
3. dive Ⓐ Ⓑ
4. bike Ⓐ Ⓑ

Listen and Fill in the blanks

1. The man with a pipe (i, p, e, p) goes on a hike (e, i, k, h)
2. A tire (r, e, t, i) is on fire (i, r, f, e)
3. Willy is flying five (e, v, f, i) kites (i, k, e, t).

16

Listen, Read and Play

Tomorrow is Children's Day!

Koko: Let's have some fun tomorrow!
Bobo: Let's ride our bikes.
Koko: Sure, and let's go on a hike!
Bobo: It will be hot, so we can dive into a lake!
Koko: Yes! We can dive five times!
Bobo: And we can fly a kite!
Koko: Yes! Then, you can help me clean my dad's pipe!
Bobo: Uh...that doesn't sound fun..

Write the words with long /i/ sound in the story.

bike, hike, dive, five, kite, pipe

Good Job!!!

17

Review

1 Listen and write the letter.

l a k e, b e e, f i v e, b a k e, m e a t, h i k e

2 Listen and circle the correct word.

race / rece / rice — seat / seet / seit — bake / beke / bike
cane / cene / cine — peach / peech / peich — kate / kete / kite

18

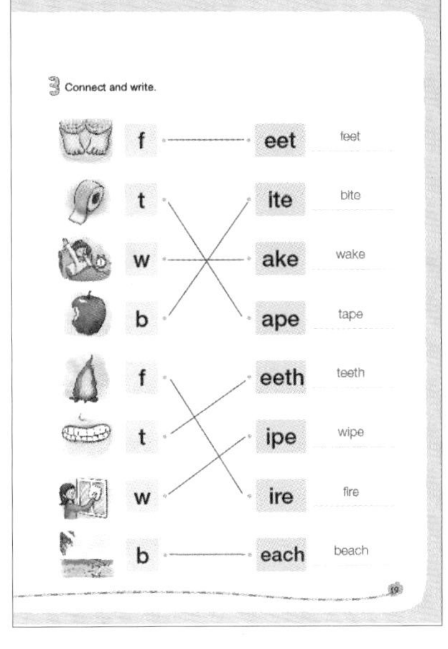

3 Connect and write.

f	eet	feet
t	ite	bite
w	ake	wake
b	ape	tape
f	eeth	teeth
t	ipe	wipe
w	ire	fire
b	each	beach

19

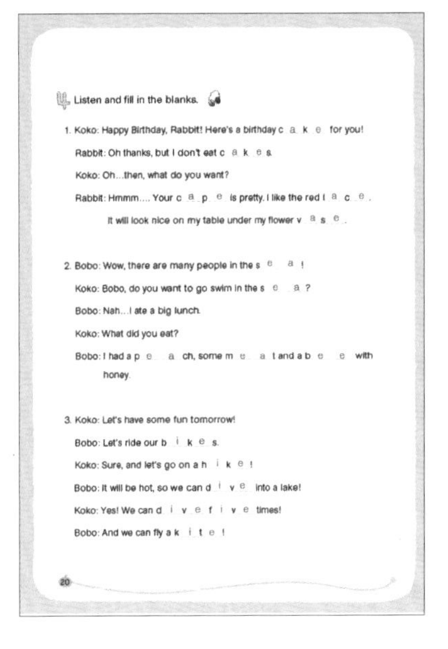

4 Listen and fill in the blanks.

1. Koko: Happy Birthday, Rabbit! Here's a birthday c a k e for you!
   Rabbit: Oh thanks, but I don't eat c a k e s.
   Koko: Oh...then, what do you want?
   Rabbit: Hmmm.... Your c a p e is pretty. I like the red l a c e.
   It will look nice on my table under my flower v a s e.
2. Bobo: Wow, there are many people in the s e a !
   Koko: Bobo, do you want to go swim in the s e a ?
   Bobo: Nah...I ate a big lunch.
   Koko: What did you eat?
   Bobo: I had a p e a ch, some m e a t and a b e e with honey.
3. Koko: Let's have some fun tomorrow!
   Bobo: Let's ride our b i k e s.
   Koko: Sure, and let's go on a h i k e !
   Bobo: It will be hot, so we can d i v e into a lake!
   Koko: Yes! We can d i v e f i v e times!
   Bobo: And we can fly a k i t e !

20

Let's Play A Game

Play a game with your partner. Use a dice and picture cards(A set).

How to Play:

1. Turn all the picture cards upside down and pile them up.
2. Take turns throwing a dice.
3. Draw a card from the deck and read the card.
4. If you can read the card, you score the number that your dice indicates. If you can't read, you do not score any.
5. The winner is the one who gets the highest score.

21

Unit 4 Long Vowel Oo

Emma's friend, Popo, wants a toy house for his birthday.

-o-e hole mole hope rope nose

rose dome home bone cone

22

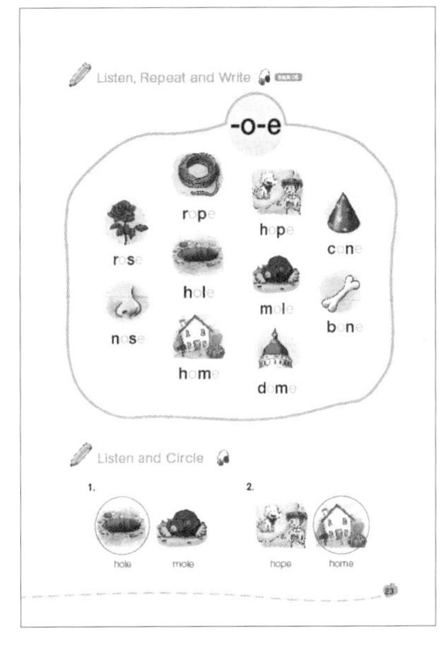

Listen, Repeat and Write

-o-e

rope, hope, rose, cone, hole, mole, nose, bone, home, dome

Listen and Circle

1. hole mole
2. hope home

23

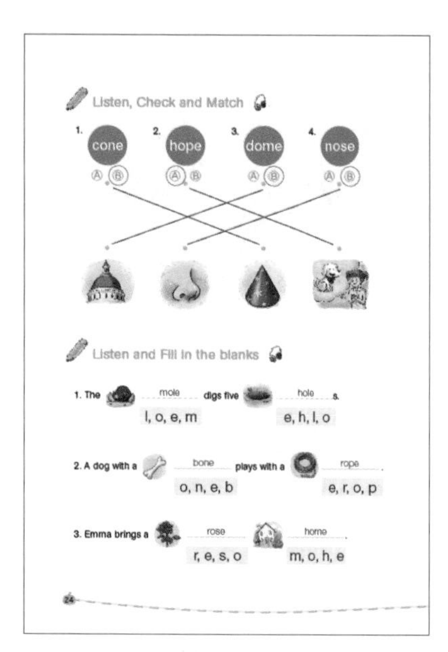

Listen, Check and Match

1. cone 2. hope 3. dome 4. nose

Listen and Fill in the blanks

1. The mole digs five hole s.
l, o, e, m — e, h, l, o

2. A dog with a bone plays with a rope.
o, n, e, b — e, r, o, p

3. Emma brings a rose home.
r, e, s, o — m, o, h, e

24

Listen, Read and Play

Koko and Bobo find a hole in the rose garden.

Bobo: Look! There is a hole.
Koko: Oh no! Let's cover the hole with dirt!
Bobo: Oh wait. Look! I see a nose!
Koko: It's a mole!
Bobo: The hole is a mole's home!
Koko: I want to live in a hole, too!
Bobo: Really? I will dig a big hole for you!

Write the words with long /o/ sound in the story.

hole, rose, nose, mole, home

Good Job!!!

25

Unit 5 Long Vowel Uu

Willy and his father are in the living room. They are busy.

-u-e
-ui-

cube tube dune June flute
fuse mule juice fruit suit

26

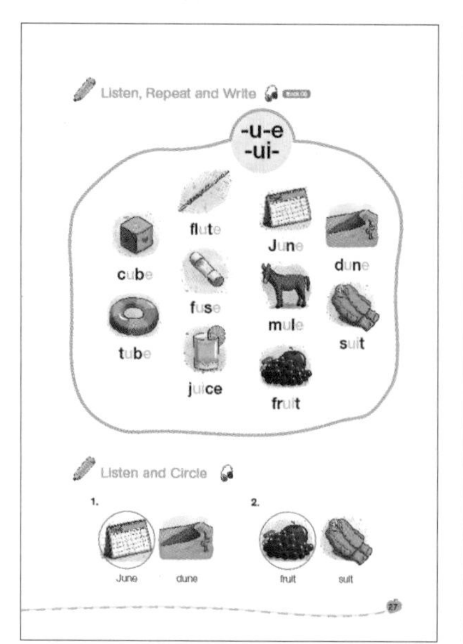

Listen, Repeat and Write

-u-e
-ui-

flute cube June dune fuse mule tube suit juice fruit

Listen and Circle

1. June dune
2. fruit suit

27

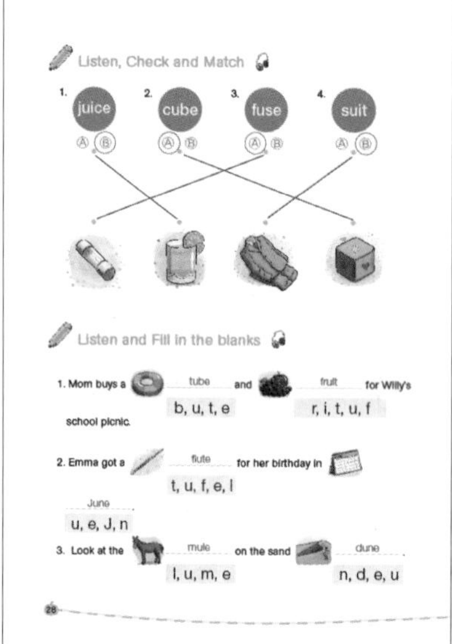

Listen, Check and Match

1. juice 2. cube 3. fuse 4. suit

Listen and Fill in the blanks

1. Mom buys a tube and fruit for Willy's school picnic.
b, u, t, e — r, i, t, u, f

2. Emma got a flute for her birthday in June.
t, u, f, e, l — u, e, J, n

3. Look at the mule on the sand dune.
l, u, m, e — n, d, e, u

28

Listen, Read and Play

Koko has a dream about a mule.
The mule is on a dune. It is a very hot day.
The mule looks thirsty.

Koko: Are you thirsty?
(Then, Koko's mom shouts.)
Mom: Wake up, Koko! Drink your orange juice with ice cubes!
Koko: Mule, do you want some orange juice with ice cubes...?
Mom: Wake up, Koko! It's time to go to your flute lesson!
Koko: Mule...it's time to go to your flute lesson...

Write the words with long /u/ sound in the story.

mule, dune, juice, cube, flute

Good Job!!!

29

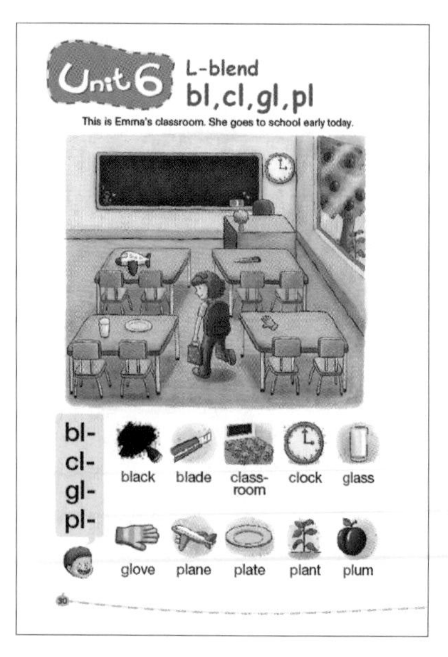

Unit 6 L-blend bl, cl, gl, pl

This is Emma's classroom. She goes to school early today.

bl-
cl-
gl-
pl-

black blade class-room clock glass
glove plane plate plant plum

30

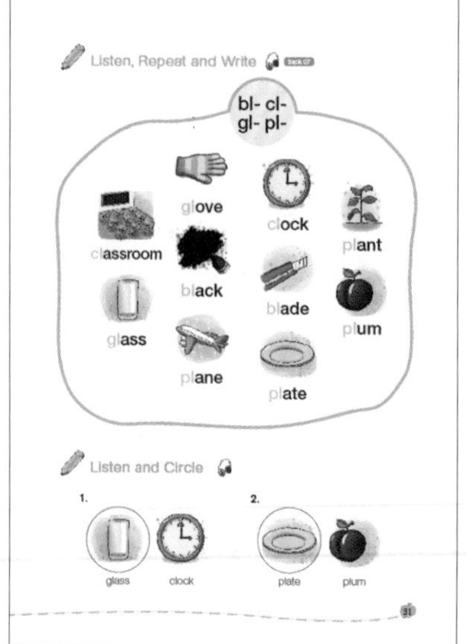

Listen, Repeat and Write

bl- cl-
gl- pl-

glove clock plant classroom black blade plum glass plane plate

Listen and Circle

1. glass clock
2. plate plum

31

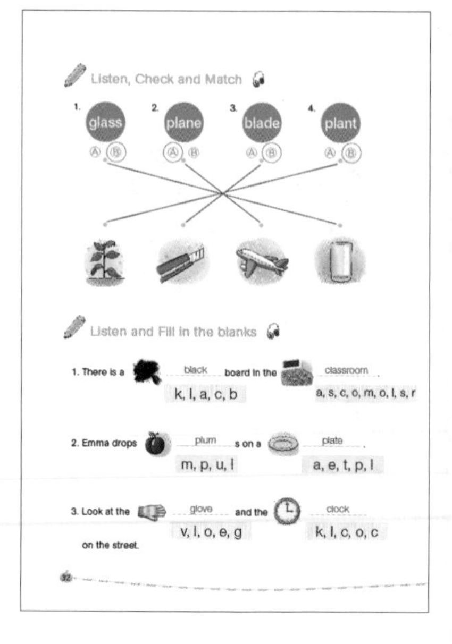

Listen, Check and Match

1. glass 2. plane 3. blade 4. plant

Listen and Fill in the blanks

1. There is a black board in the classroom.
k, l, a, c, b — a, s, c, o, m, o, l, s, r

2. Emma drops plum s on a plate.
m, p, u, l — a, e, t, p, l

3. Look at the glove and the clock on the street.
v, l, o, e, g — k, l, c, o, c

32

Listen, Read and Play

It was Koko's first day of school.

Koko comes home and sits with her mom.

Mom: How was school?

Koko: It was great, mom. I did many things!

Mom: Really? Tell me more, Koko.

Koko: I wrote on the blackboard. I wrote on my desk.

I broke the classroom clock.

And I ate all the plums from the plum tree!

Mom: Oh...no, Koko.

Write the words with /bl/, /cl/, /gl/ and /pl/ sound in the story.

black, classroom, clock, plum

Good Job!!!

Review

1 Listen and write the letter.

d o m e | s u i t | g l a s s

n o s e | j u i c e | p l a n e

2 Listen and circle the correct word.

hape / hope / hepe — flate / flote / flute — black / block / bluck

hame / hume / home — Jone / June / Jane — clack / clock / cluck

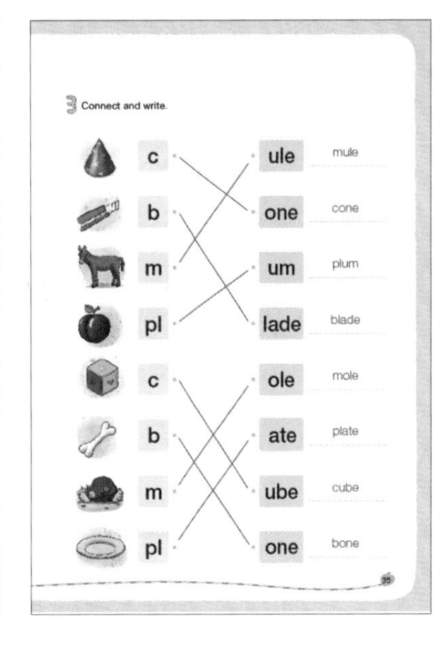

3 Connect and write.

c	ule	mule
b	one	cone
m	um	plum
pl	lade	blade
c	ole	mole
b	ate	plate
m	ube	cube
pl	one	bone

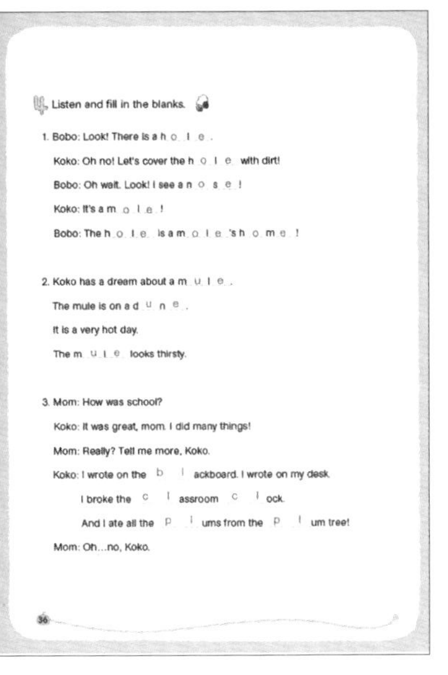

4 Listen and fill in the blanks.

1. Bobo: Look! There is a h o l e .

Koko: Oh no! Let's cover the h o l e with dirt!

Bobo: Oh wait. Look! I see a n o s e !

Koko: It's a m o l e !

Bobo: The h o l e is a m o l e 's h o m e !

2. Koko has a dreem about a m u l e .

The mule is on a d u n e .

It is a very hot day.

The m u l e looks thirsty.

3. Mom: How was school?

Koko: It was great, mom. I did many things!

Mom: Really? Tell me more, Koko.

Koko: I wrote on the b l ackboard. I wrote on my desk.

I broke the c l assroom c l ock.

And I ate all the p l ums from the p l um tree!

Mom: Oh...no, Koko.

Let's Play A Game

Play tic-tac-toe game with your partner.

r__p__	m__l__	s__t	___ack
___ate	___ass	___ant	b__n__
j___ce	___ade	___ock	___ove
___um	n__s__	J__n__	___ane

How to Play

1. Choose a square.
2. Say the name of the picture that you chose. Then, complete the word.
3. When you complete the word, put a check mark on the picture. If you can't, do not put a check mark.
4. Take turns choosing squares and continue the game.
5. The one who gets four in a row wins.

Unit 7 R-blend br, dr, pr, tr

Emma and Willy are at a toy shop on Nexus street.

br- dr- pr- tr-

bread brush brick bride dress

drum price prince train truck

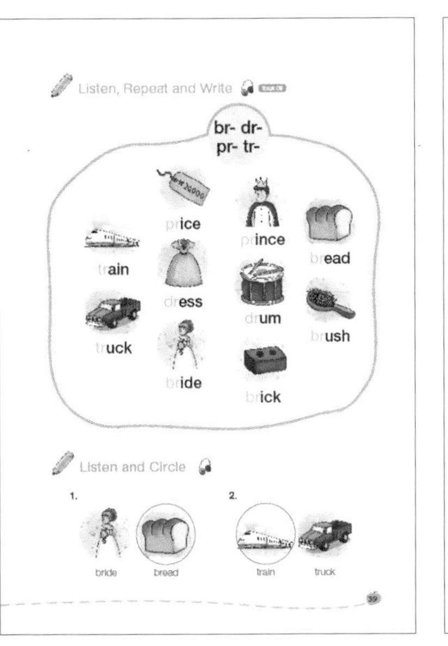

Listen, Repeat and Write

br- dr- pr- tr-

price, prince, train, bread, dress, drum, truck, brush, bride, brick

Listen and Circle

1. bride bread

2. train truck

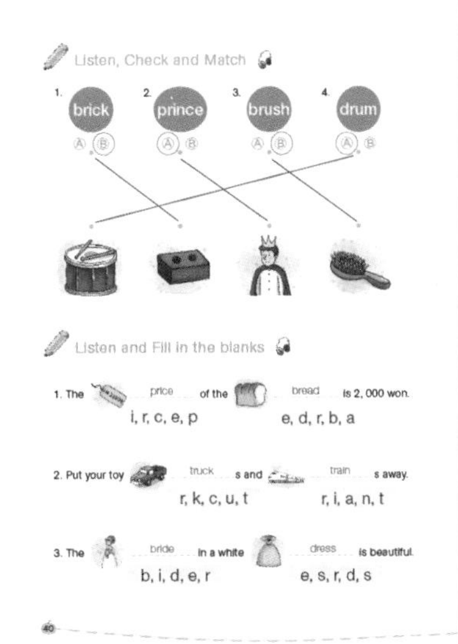

Listen, Check and Match

1. brick 2. prince 3. brush 4. drum

Listen and Fill in the blanks

1. The price of the bread is 2, 000 won.

i, r, c, e, p — e, d, r, b, a

2. Put your toy truck s and train s away.

r, k, c, u, t — r, i, a, n, t

3. The bride in a white dress is beautiful.

b, i, d, e, r — e, s, r, d, s

Listen, Read and Play

Koko and Bobo are at a toyshop.

There are lots of toys.

Koko: Look! It's a doll with a bride's dress!

(Bobo plays the drum. He can't hear Koko.)

Do you want to brush her hair, Bobo?

Bobo: What? No! I don't want to play with the truck and the train.

Koko: No-no. Do you want to play with my doll?

Bobo: What? No! I don't want to play with the door!

Write the words with /br/, /dr/, /pr/ and /tr/ sound in the story.

bride, dress, drum, brush, truck, train

Good Job!!!

Unit 8 S-blend sm, sn, sp, st

Emma and Willy are in a ghost house. It is dark and scary.

sm- sn- sp- st-

smell smile snail snake spider

spot stone stop store stove

42

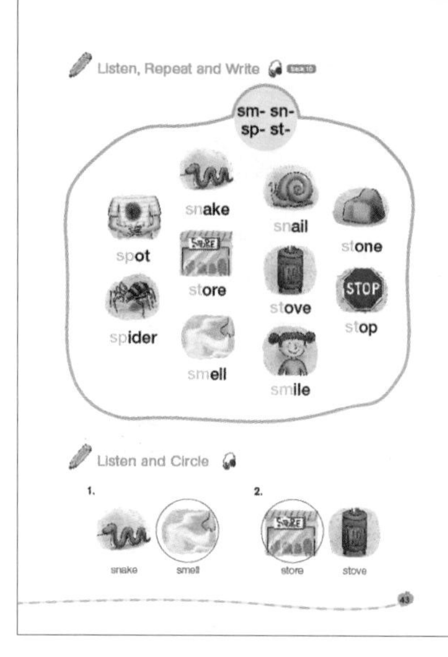

Listen, Repeat and Write

sm- sn- sp- st-

spot snake store spider smell snail stove smile stone stop

Listen and Circle

1. snake smell

2. store stove

43

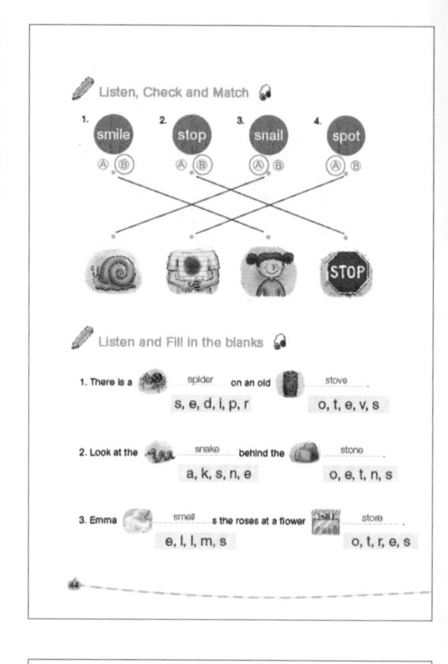

Listen, Check and Match

1. smile Ⓐ Ⓑ 2. stop Ⓐ Ⓑ 3. snail Ⓐ Ⓑ 4. spot Ⓐ Ⓑ

Listen and Fill in the blanks

1. There is a spider on an old stove.
s, e, d, i, p, r o, t, e, v, s

2. Look at the snake behind the stone.
a, k, s, n, e o, e, t, n, s

3. Emma smells the roses at a flower store.
e, l, l, m, s o, t, r, e, s

44

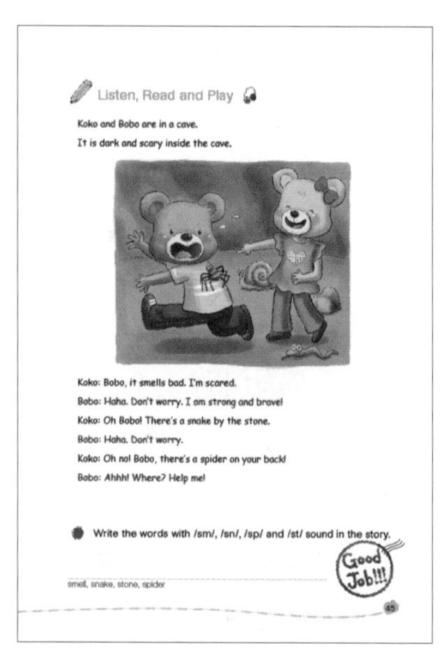

Listen, Read and Play

Koko and Bobo are in a cave.
It is dark and scary inside the cave.

Koko: Bobo, it smells bad. I'm scared.
Bobo: Haha. Don't worry. I am strong and brave!
Koko: Oh Bobo! There's a snake by the stone.
Bobo: Haha. Don't worry.
Koko: Oh no! Bobo, there's a spider on your back!
Bobo: Ahhh! Where? Help me!

Write the words with /sm/, /sn/, /sp/ and /st/ sound in the story.

smell, snake, stone, spider

Good Job!!!

45

Unit 9 Ending-blend nd, ng, nk, nt

Emma's family goes camping in the woods.

-nd -ng -nk -nt

land pond sing wing long

ring drink wink ant tent

46

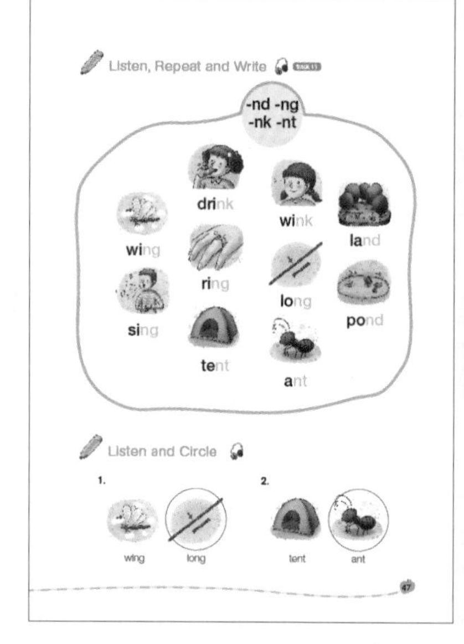

Listen, Repeat and Write

-nd -ng -nk -nt

wing sing drink ring tent wink long ant land pond

Listen and Circle

1. wing long

2. tent ant

47

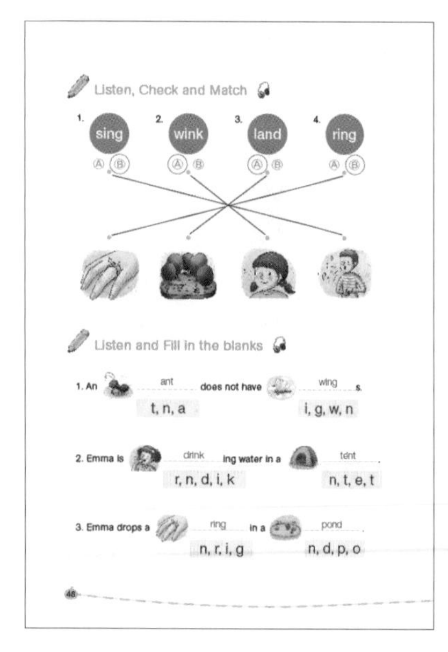

Listen, Check and Match

1. sing Ⓐ Ⓑ 2. wink Ⓐ Ⓑ 3. land Ⓐ Ⓑ 4. ring Ⓐ Ⓑ

Listen and Fill in the blanks

1. An ant does not have wings.
t, n, a i, g, w, n

2. Emma is drinking water in a tent.
r, n, d, i, k n, t, e, t

3. Emma drops a ring in a pond.
n, r, i, g n, d, p, o

48

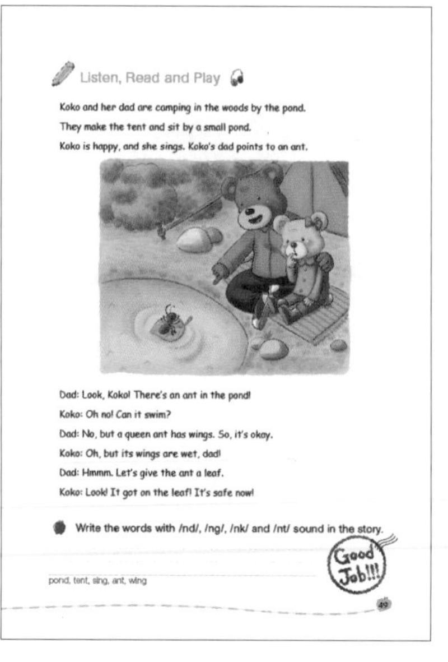

Listen, Read and Play

Koko and her dad are camping in the woods by the pond.
They make the tent and sit by a small pond.
Koko is happy, and she sings. Koko's dad points to an ant.

Dad: Look, Koko! There's an ant in the pond!
Koko: Oh no! Can it swim?
Dad: No, but a queen ant has wings. So, it's okay.
Koko: Oh, but its wings are wet, dad!
Dad: Hmmm. Let's give the ant a leaf.
Koko: Look! It got on the leaf! It's safe now!

Write the words with /nd/, /ng/, /nk/ and /nt/ sound in the story.

pond, tent, sing, ant, wing

Good Job!!!

49

Review

1 Listen and write the letter.

brick smile sing

drum stop ring

2 Listen and circle the correct word.

brush / drush / prush — small / snail / spail — land / lang / lank

brince / drince / prince — snot / smot / spot — wind / wing / wink

50

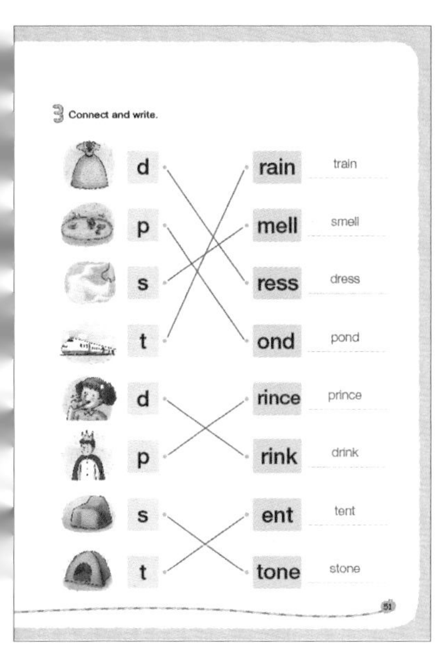
3 Connect and write.
d
p
s
t
d
p
s
t
rain
train
mell
smell
ress
dress
ond
pond
rince
prince
rink
drink
ent
tent
tone
stone
51

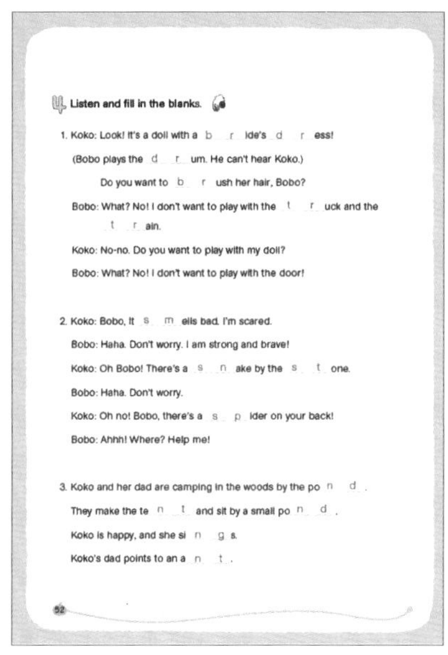
4 Listen and fill in the blanks.
1. Koko: Look! It's a doll with a b r ide's d r ess!
(Bobo plays the d r um. He can't hear Koko.)
Do you want to b r ush her hair, Bobo?
Bobo: What? No! I don't want to play with the t r uck and the t r ain.
Koko: No-no. Do you want to play with my doll?
Bobo: What? No! I don't want to play with the door!
2. Koko: Bobo, It s m ells bad. I'm scared.
Bobo: Haha. Don't worry. I am strong and brave!
Koko: Oh Bobo! There's a s n ake by the s t one.
Bobo: Haha. Don't worry.
Koko: Oh no! Bobo, there's a s p ider on your back!
Bobo: Ahhh! Where? Help me!
3. Koko and her dad are camping in the woods by the po n d .
They make the te n t and sit by a small po n d .
Koko is happy, and she si n g s.
Koko's dad points to an a n t .
52

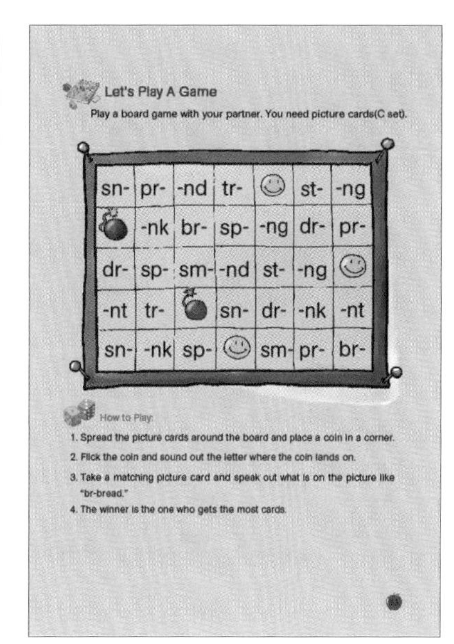
Let's Play A Game
Play a board game with your partner. You need picture cards(C set).
sn- pr- -nd tr- st- -ng
-nk br- sp- -ng dr- pr-
dr- sp- sm- -nd st- -ng
-nt tr- sn- dr- -nk -nt
sn- -nk sp- sm- pr- br-
How to Play
1. Spread the picture cards around the board and place a coin in a corner.
2. Flick the coin and sound out the letter where the coin lands on.
3. Take a matching picture card and speak out what is on the picture like "br-bread."
4. The winner is the one who gets the most cards.

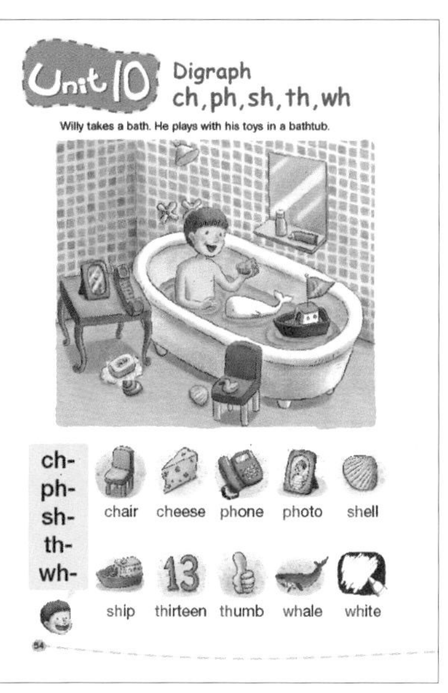
Unit 10
Digraph
ch, ph, sh, th, wh
Willy takes a bath. He plays with his toys in a bathtub.
ch-
ph-
sh-
th-
wh-
chair
cheese
phone
photo
shell
ship
thirteen
thumb
whale
white
54

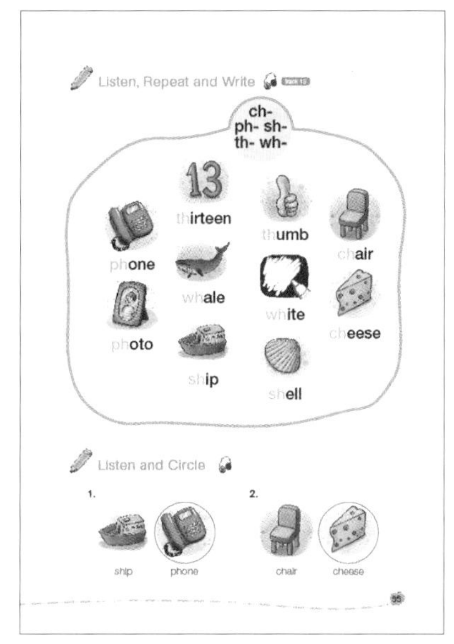
Listen, Repeat and Write
ch-
ph- sh-
th- wh-
thirteen
thumb
chair
phone
whale
white
photo
cheese
ship
shell
Listen and Circle
1.
ship
phone
2.
chair
cheese
55

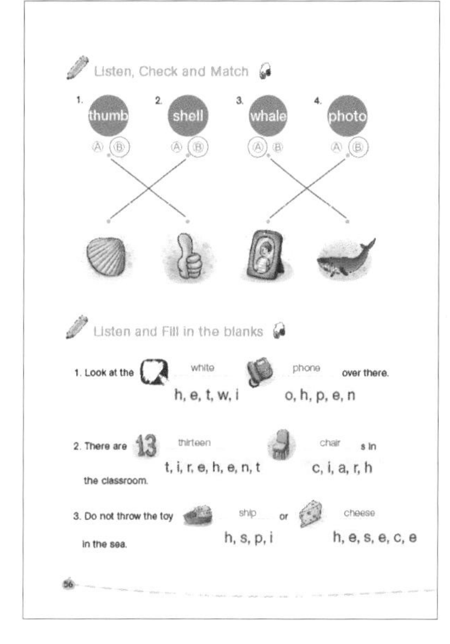
Listen, Check and Match
1. thumb
2. shell
3. whale
4. photo
Listen and Fill in the blanks
1. Look at the white phone over there.
h, e, t, w, i
o, h, p, e, n
2. There are thirteen chairs in the classroom.
t, i, r, e, h, e, n, t
c, i, a, r, h
3. Do not throw the toy ship or cheese in the sea.
h, s, p, i
h, e, s, e, c, e
56

Listen, Read and Play
Koko meets her sea friends.
A shell and a white whale sit in their chairs.
Shell: Koko, I want to visit your house.
Koko: Sure, but how can we go?
Whale: Hmmm... We can take the ship!
Shell: How long will it take? What do we eat?
Koko: It will take thirteen days!
And I have some cheese in my pocket. We can eat cheese!
Shell and Whale: Thirteen days with only cheese? No way!
Write the words with /ch/, /ph/, /sh/, /th/ and /wh/ sound in the story.
shell, white, whale, chair, ship, thirteen, cheese
Good Job!!!
57

Unit 11
Double Letter Vowels
oa, ow
This is Emma's room. She is going outside.
-oa-
-ow
boat
coat
goat
soap
toast
bowl
pillow
snow
window
yellow
58

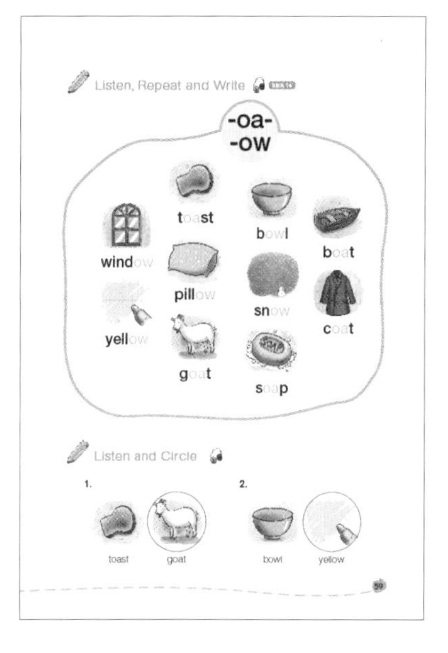
Listen, Repeat and Write
-oa-
-ow
toast
bowl
window
boat
pillow
snow
coat
yellow
goat
soap
Listen and Circle
1.
toast
goat
2.
bowl
yellow
59

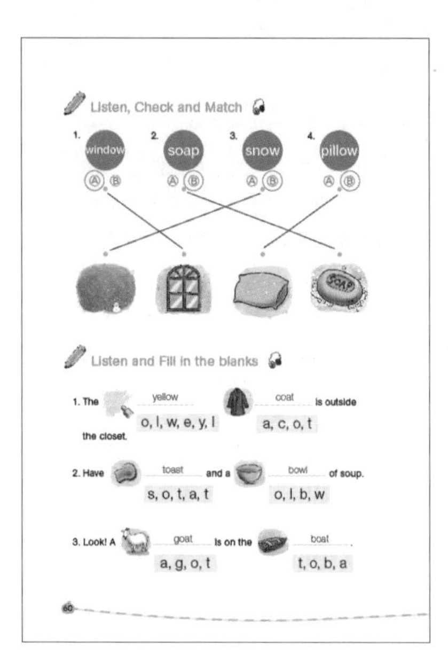
Listen, Check and Match

1. window Ⓐ Ⓑ 2. soap Ⓐ Ⓑ 3. snow Ⓐ Ⓑ 4. pillow Ⓐ Ⓑ

Listen and Fill in the blanks

1. The yellow (o, l, w, e, y, l) coat (a, c, o, t) is outside the closet.

2. Have toast (s, o, t, a, t) and a bowl (o, l, b, w) of soup.

3. Look! A goat (a, g, o, t) is on the boat (t, o, b, a).

60

Listen, Read and Play

Bobo comes over to Koko's house. Bobo wants to play outside in the snow. But, Koko cannot find her hairbrush!

Koko: Is it next to the toy boat?
Bobo: No, it's not here!
Koko: Then, is it behind the toy goat?
Bobo: No, it's not there!
Koko: Look under the yellow pillow, Bobo!
Bobo: No, it's not here. Oh wait! It's on the bed!
Koko: Ah-ha! Great! Now, let's go play outside!
Bobo: But... what about your room? It's very dirty.

Write the words with /oa/ and /ow/ sound in the story.

snow, boat, goat, yellow, pillow

Good Job!!!

61

Unit 12 Double Letter Vowels oi, oy

Willy and Emma are in a playroom at a toy shop.

-oi- -oy(-)

boil soil coil coin point

toilet boy joy toy oyster

62

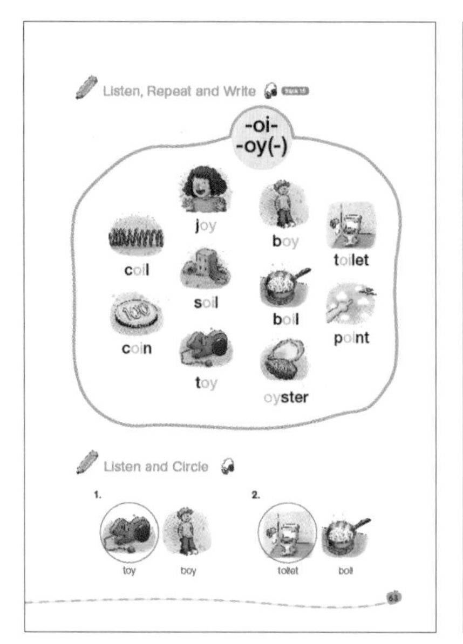
Listen, Repeat and Write

-oi- -oy(-)

joy boy toilet coil soil boil coin point toy oyster

Listen and Circle

1. toy boy

2. toilet boil

63

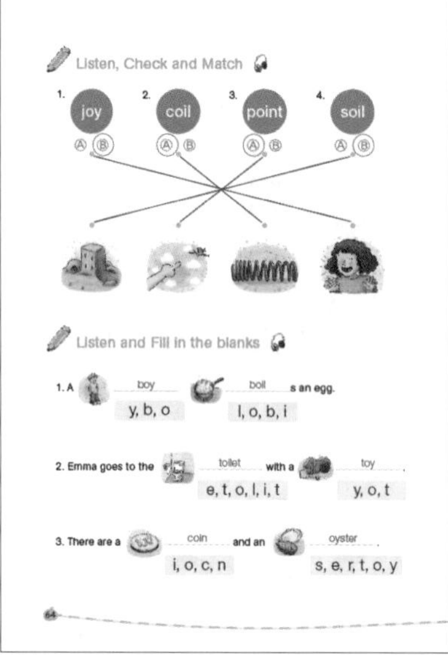
Listen, Check and Match

1. joy Ⓐ Ⓑ 2. coil Ⓐ Ⓑ 3. point Ⓐ Ⓑ 4. soil Ⓐ Ⓑ

Listen and Fill in the blanks

1. A boy (y, b, o) boil (l, o, b, i) s an egg.

2. Emma goes to the toilet (e, t, o, l, i, t) with a toy (y, o, t).

3. There are a coin (i, o, c, n) and an oyster (s, e, r, t, o, y).

64

Listen, Read and Play

Bobo wants to play in the sandbox.
But a boy is there. He's making a sandcastle.

Bobo: Can I play with you?
Boy: No. Go away.
Bobo: I will give you that toy.
(Bobo points to a toy airplane.)
Boy: No, I don't like airplanes.
(Then, a coin drops from Bobo's hand.)
Boy: Oooh! A coin! I will give you my sandcastle. I want this coin!

Write the words with /oi/ and /oy/ sound in the story.

boy, toy, point, coin

Good Job!!!

65

Review

1 Listen and write the letter.

ship window point
photo soil joy

2 Listen and circle the correct word.

chell / shell / phell
pilloa / pillow / pilloy
coil / coal / coy
shale / thale / whale
chair / shair / whair
coat / cout / coy

66

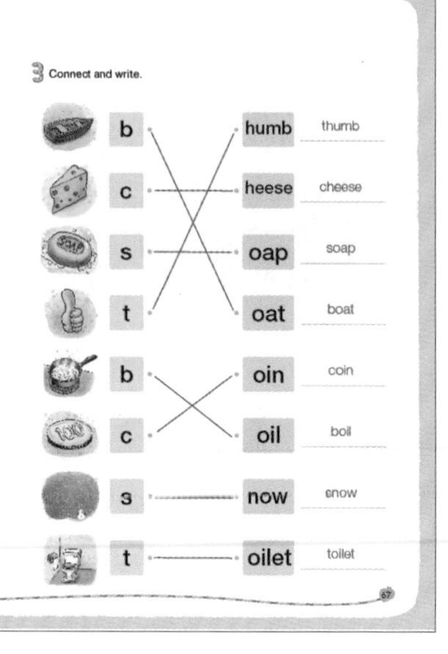
3 Connect and write.

b	humb	thumb
c	heese	cheese
s	oap	soap
t	oat	boat
b	oin	coin
c	oil	boil
s	now	snow
t	oilet	toilet

67

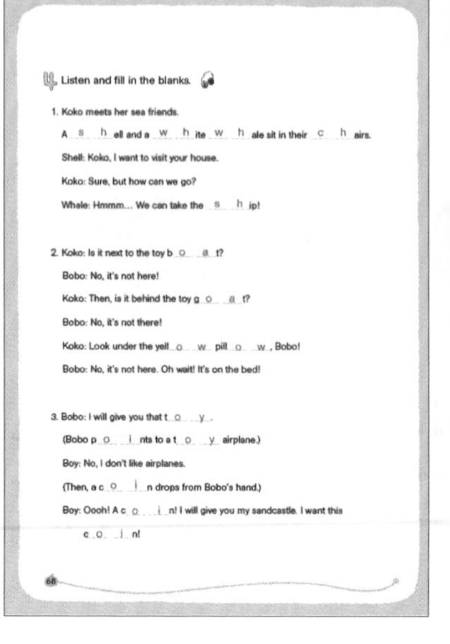
4 Listen and fill in the blanks.

1. Koko meets her sea friends.
A s h ell and a w h ite w h ale sit in their c h airs.
Shell: Koko, I want to visit your house.
Koko: Sure, but how can we go?
Whale: Hmmm... We can take the s h ip!

2. Koko: Is it next to the toy b o a t?
Bobo: No, it's not here!
Koko: Then, is it behind the toy g o a t?
Bobo: No, it's not there!
Koko: Look under the yell o w pill o w , Bobo!
Bobo: No, it's not here. Oh wait! It's on the bed!

3. Bobo: I will give you that t o y .
(Bobo p o i nts to a t o y airplane.)
Boy: No, I don't like airplanes.
(Then, a c o i n drops from Bobo's hand.)
Boy: Oooh! A c o i n! I will give you my sandcastle. I want this c o i n!

68

Let's Play A Game

Play a game with your partner.

chair. c.h.a.i.r

Chair

How to Play:

1. Make word cards using the words that you learned in Unit 10, Unit 11, Unit 12.
2. Spread the word cards that you made on the desk.
3. A teacher chooses a flash card randomly. Then the teacher reads the card out loud.
4. Listen to the word your teacher says. Then try to be the first student to touch the correct word card. The first student takes the word card.
5. The student who gets the most scores wins.

Unit 13 Double Letter Vowels ou, ow

After the party, Emma and Willy are on the way home.

-ou- -ow-

cloud loud house mouth cow

owl gown crown brown clown

70

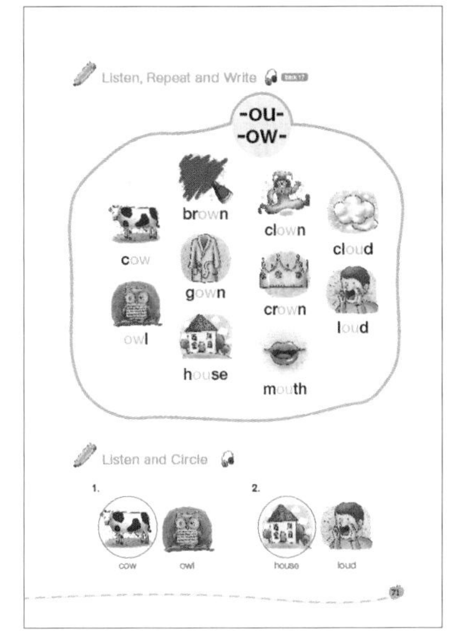
Listen, Repeat and Write

-ou- -ow-

cow brown clown cloud gown crown loud owl house mouth

Listen and Circle

1. cow owl

2. house loud

71

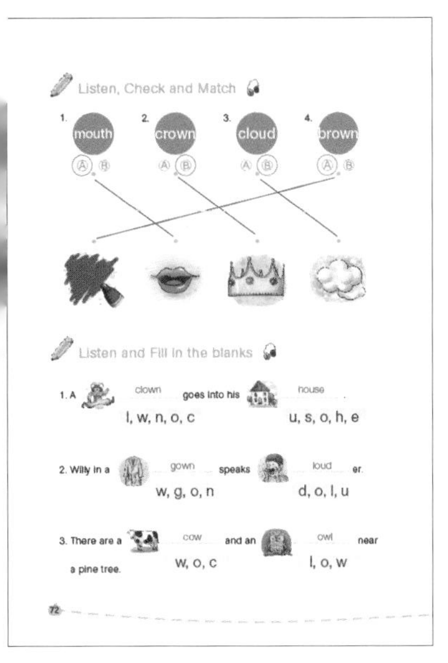
Listen, Check and Match

1. mouth 2. crown 3. cloud 4. brown

Listen and Fill in the blanks

1. A clown goes into his house. l, w, n, o, c u, s, o, h, e

2. Willy in a gown speaks louder. w, g, o, n d, o, l, u

3. There are a cow and an owl near a pine tree. w, o, c l, o, w

72

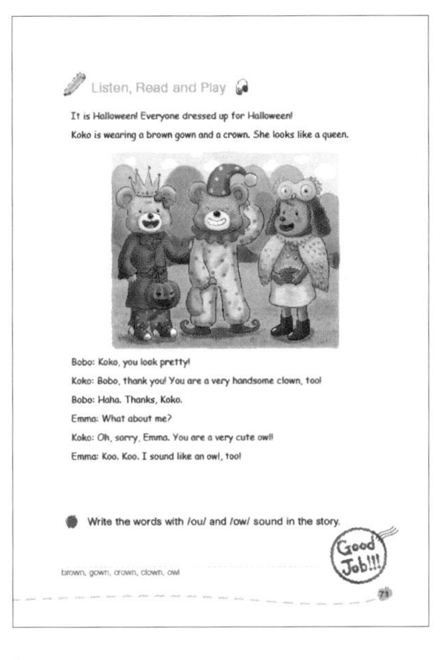
Listen, Read and Play

It is Halloween! Everyone dressed up for Halloween!

Koko is wearing a brown gown and a crown. She looks like a queen.

Bobo: Koko, you look pretty!

Koko: Bobo, thank you! You are a very handsome clown, too!

Bobo: Haha. Thanks, Koko.

Emma: What about me?

Koko: Oh, sorry, Emma. You are a very cute owl!

Emma: Koo. Koo. I sound like an owl, too!

Write the words with /ou/ and /ow/ sound in the story.

brown, gown, crown, clown, owl

Good Job!!!

73

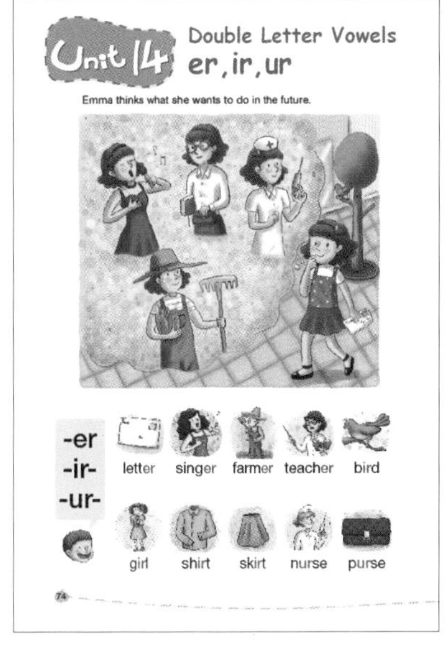
Unit 14 Double Letter Vowels er, ir, ur

Emma thinks what she wants to do in the future.

-er -ir- -ur-

letter singer farmer teacher bird

girl shirt skirt nurse purse

74

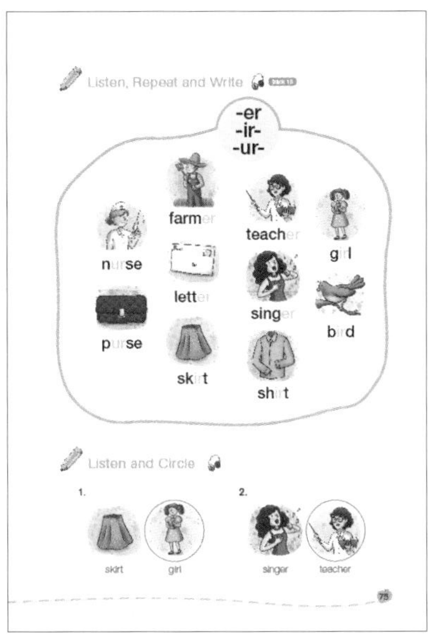
Listen, Repeat and Write

-er -ir- -ur-

farmer nurse teacher girl letter singer purse bird skirt shirt

Listen and Circle

1. skirt girl

2. singer teacher

75

Listen, Check and Match

1. farmer 2. shirt 3. bird 4. nurse

Listen and Fill in the blanks

1. A girl wears a skirt. r, l, g, i r, k, i, s, t

2. A teacher is writing a letter. t, e, c, e, a, r, h t, e, r, e, t, l

3. A singer wants to buy a purse. n, e, s, i, r, g u, s, p, e, r

76

Listen, Read and Play

Koko waits for the bus at the bus stop.

A nurse, a boy in a shirt and a girl in a skirt are at the bus stop.

BUS STOP

Nurse: Excuse me, what time is it?

Koko: Sorry, I don't know.

Boy: Excuse me, what time is it?

Koko: Sorry, I don't know.

Girl: Excuse me. You have a watch. Please tell us what time it is.

Koko: Ohhh! It's a toy watch. It's not a real watch!

Write the words with /er/, /ir/ and /ur/ sound in the story.

nurse, shirt, girl, skirt

Good Job!!!

77

Unit 15 Double Letter Vowels oo

One evening, Emma cooks some food for her mom.

-oo-

book cook food foot goose

moon pool spoon wood zoo

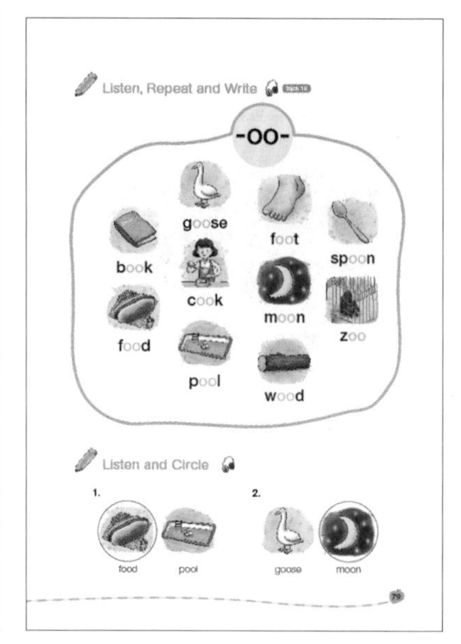
Listen, Repeat and Write

-oo-

goose foot spoon book cook moon food pool zoo wood

Listen and Circle

1. food pool

2. goose moon

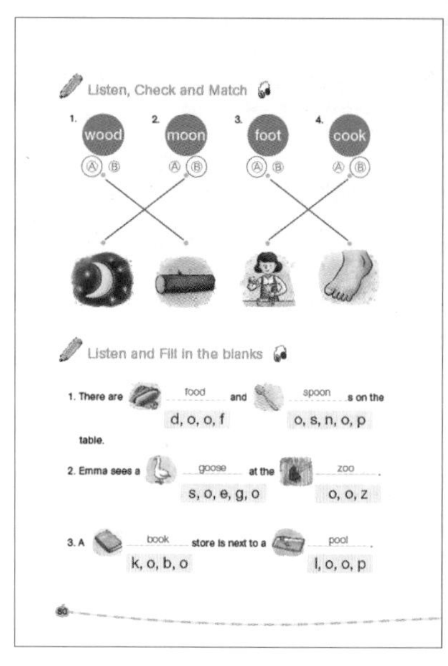
Listen, Check and Match

1. wood 2. moon 3. foot 4. cook

Listen and Fill in the blanks

1. There are food (d, o, o, f) and spoon (o, s, n, o, p) s on the table.

2. Emma sees a goose (s, o, e, g, o) at the zoo (o, o, z).

3. A book (k, o, b, o) store is next to a pool (l, o, o, p).

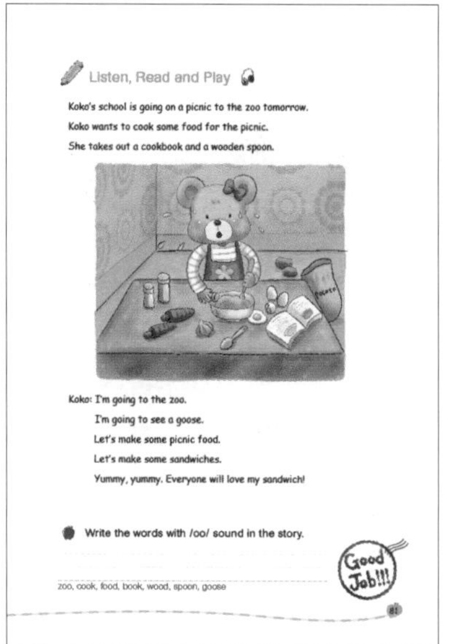
Listen, Read and Play

Koko's school is going on a picnic to the zoo tomorrow.
Koko wants to cook some food for the picnic.
She takes out a cookbook and a wooden spoon.

Koko: I'm going to the zoo.
I'm going to see a goose.
Let's make some picnic food.
Let's make some sandwiches.
Yummy, yummy. Everyone will love my sandwich!

Write the words with /oo/ sound in the story.

zoo, cook, food, book, wood, spoon, goose

Good Job!!!

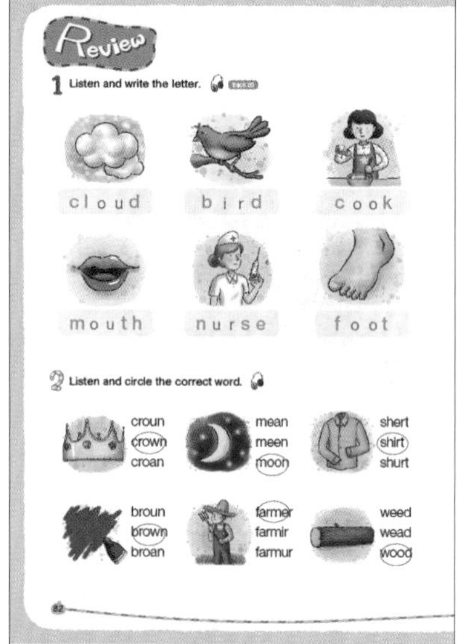
Review

1 Listen and write the letter.

cloud bird cook mouth nurse foot

2 Listen and circle the correct word.

croun crown croan | mean meen moon | shert shirt shurt

broun brown broan | farmer farmir farmur | weed wead wood

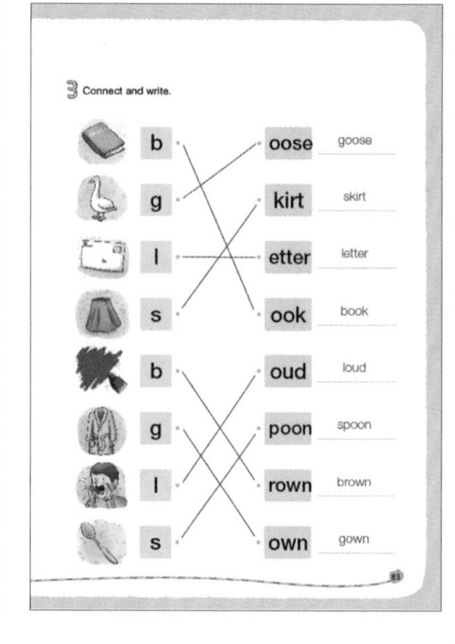
3 Connect and write.

b oose goose
g kirt skirt
l etter letter
s ook book
b oud loud
g poon spoon
l rown brown
s own gown

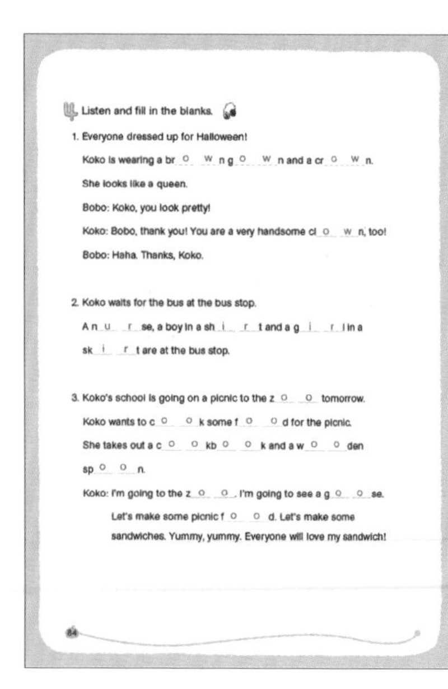
4 Listen and fill in the blanks.

1. Everyone dressed up for Halloween!
Koko is wearing a brown gown and a crown.
She looks like a queen.
Bobo: Koko, you look pretty!
Koko: Bobo, thank you! You are a very handsome clown, too!
Bobo: Haha. Thanks, Koko.

2. Koko waits for the bus at the bus stop.
A nurse, a boy in a shirt and a girl in a skirt are at the bus stop.

3. Koko's school is going on a picnic to the zoo tomorrow.
Koko wants to cook some food for the picnic.
She takes out a cookbook and a wooden spoon.
Koko: I'm going to the zoo. I'm going to see a goose.
Let's make some picnic food. Let's make some sandwiches. Yummy, yummy. Everyone will love my sandwich!

Let's Play A Game

Play a game with your partner.

How to Play

1. Make a dice from the appendix.
2. Take turns throwing the dice.
3. Make a word that has the sound on the dice. For example, if your dice shows "ou", make a word that has "ou" sound like "cloud."
4. If you make a correct word, you get 5 points. If you can't, you lose 3 points.
5. The winner is the one who gets the most scores.

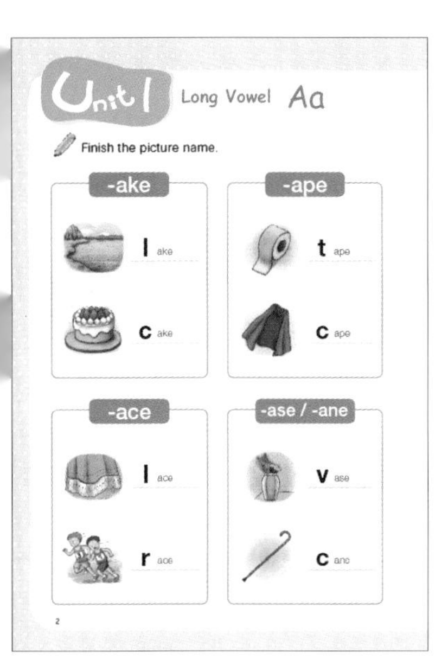

Unit 1 Long Vowel Aa

Finish the picture name.

-ake: l ake, c ake

-ape: t ape, c ape

-ace: l ace, r ace

-ase / -ane: v ase, c ane

2

Choose the correct word and write it.

wake — wake / wave
bake — base / bake
vase — vape / vase
cake — cake / cale
race — race / rake
cane — cane / case

3

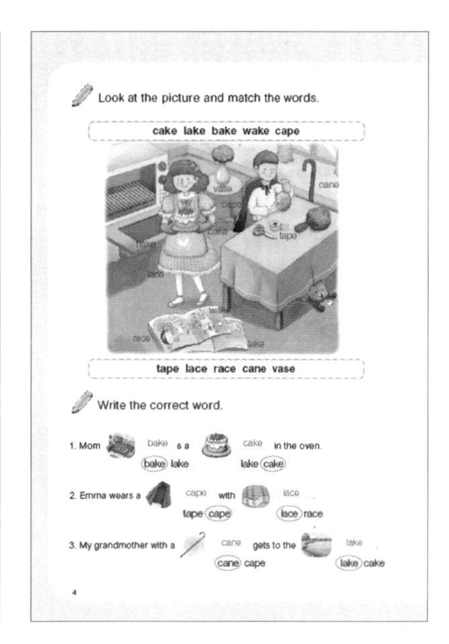

Look at the picture and match the words.

cake lake bake wake cape

tape lace race cane vase

Write the correct word.

1. Mom bake s a cake in the oven. (bake / lake) (lake / cake)

2. Emma wears a cape with lace. (tape / cape) (lace / race)

3. My grandmother with a cane gets to the lake. (cane / cape) (lake / cake)

4

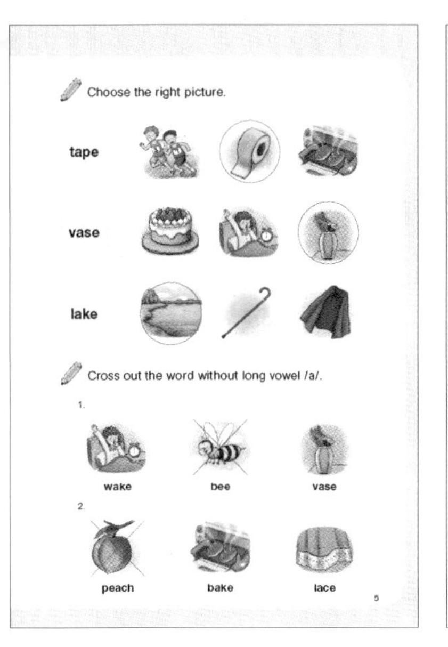

Choose the right picture.

tape

vase

lake

Cross out the word without long vowel /a/.

1. wake bee vase

2. peach bake lace

5

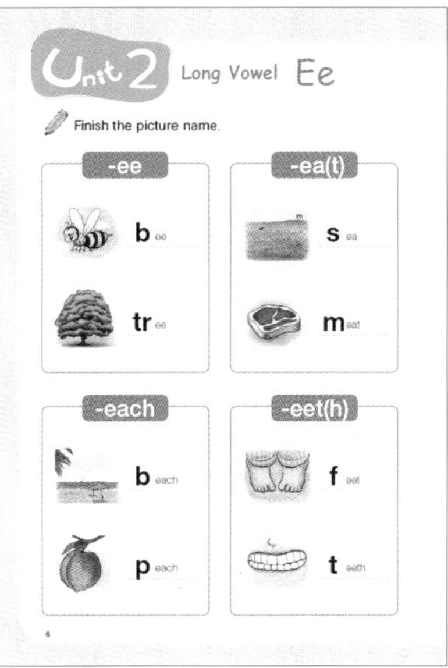

Unit 2 Long Vowel Ee

Finish the picture name.

-ee: b ee, tr ee

-ea(t): s ea, m eat

-each: b each, p each

-eet(h): f eet, t eeth

6

Choose the correct word and write it.

feet — feet / feat
tea — tea / tee
meat — meet / meat
bee — bea / bee
beach — beech / beach
seat — seat / seet

7

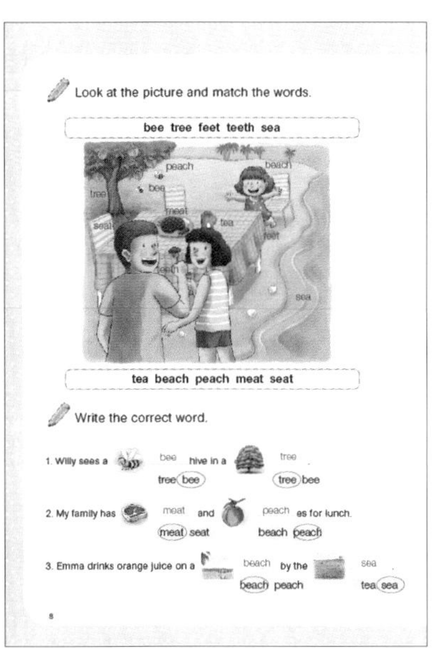

Look at the picture and match the words.

bee tree feet teeth sea

tea beach peach meat seat

Write the correct word.

1. Willy sees a bee hive in a tree. (tree / bee) (tree / bee)

2. My family has meat and peach as for lunch. (meat / seat) (beach / peach)

3. Emma drinks orange juice on a beach by the sea. (beach / peach) (tea / sea)

8

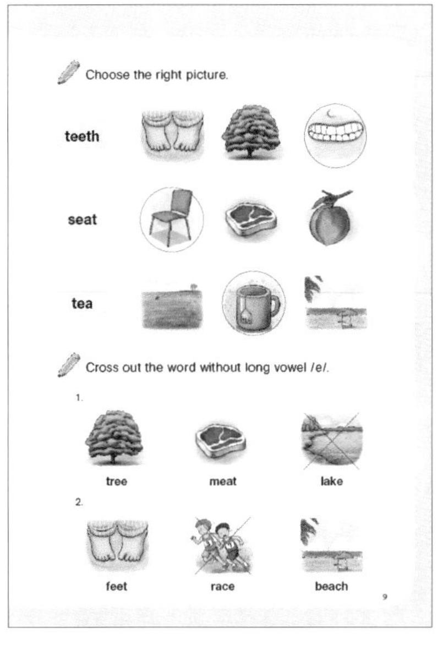

Choose the right picture.

teeth

seat

tea

Cross out the word without long vowel /e/.

1. tree meat lake

2. feet race beach

9

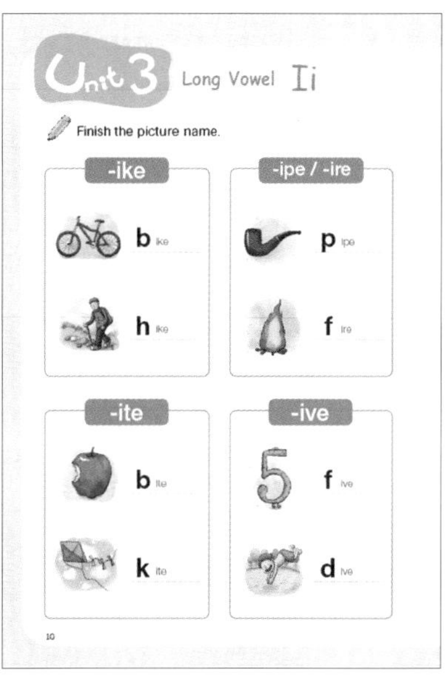

Unit 3 Long Vowel Ii

Finish the picture name.

-ike: b ike, h ike

-ipe / -ire: p ipe, f ire

-ite: b ite, k ite

-ive: f ive, d ive

10

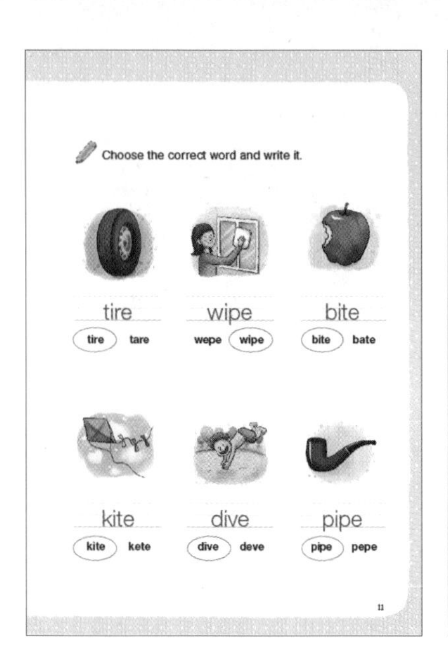

Choose the correct word and write it.

tire — tire / tare
wipe — wepe / wipe
bite — bite / bate
kite — kite / kete
dive — dive / deve
pipe — pipe / pepe

11

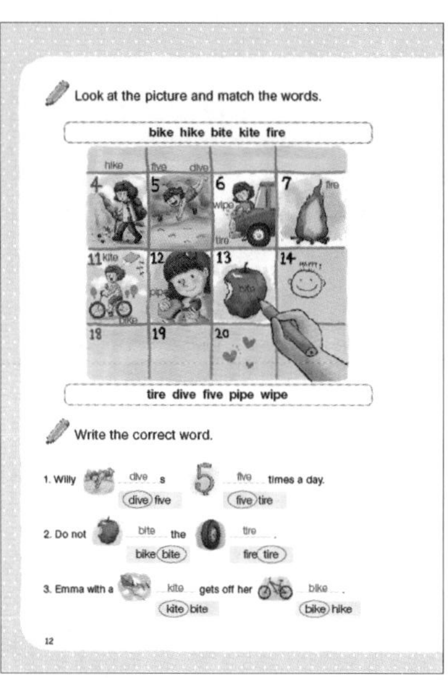

Look at the picture and match the words.

bike hike bite kite fire

tire dive five pipe wipe

Write the correct word.

1. Willy dive s five times a day. (dive / five) (five / tire)
2. Do not bite the tire. (bike / bite) (fire / tire)
3. Emma with a kite gets off her bike. (kite / bite) (bike / hike)

12

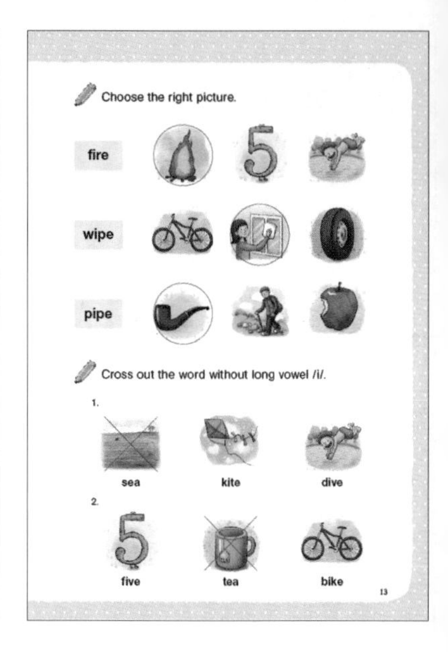

Choose the right picture.

fire

wipe

pipe

Cross out the word without long vowel /i/.

1. sea kite dive
2. five tea bike

13

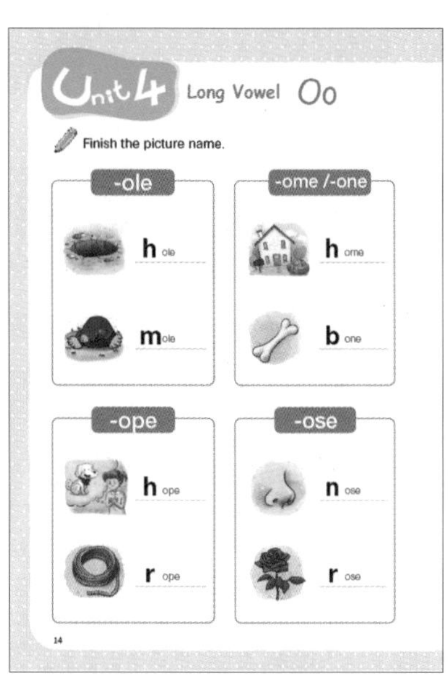

Unit 4 Long Vowel Oo

Finish the picture name.

-ole: h ole, m ole
-ome / -one: h ome, b one
-ope: h ope, r ope
-ose: n ose, r ose

14

Choose the correct word and write it.

dome — dome / dame
home — home / hame
rose — rose / rase
bone — bone / bane
nose — nose / nase
cone — cone / cane

15

Look at the picture and match the words.

hole mole hope rope nose

rose dome home bone cone

Write the correct word.

1. What a beautiful home and a rose garden! (home / dome) (nose / rose)
2. There is a big hole near the bone in the backyard. (mole / hole) (bone / cone)
3. A mole jumps a rope. (mole / hole) (rope / hope)

16

Choose the right picture.

cone

nose

hope

Cross out the word without long vowel /o/.

1. bone wipe mole
2. hike rope dome

17

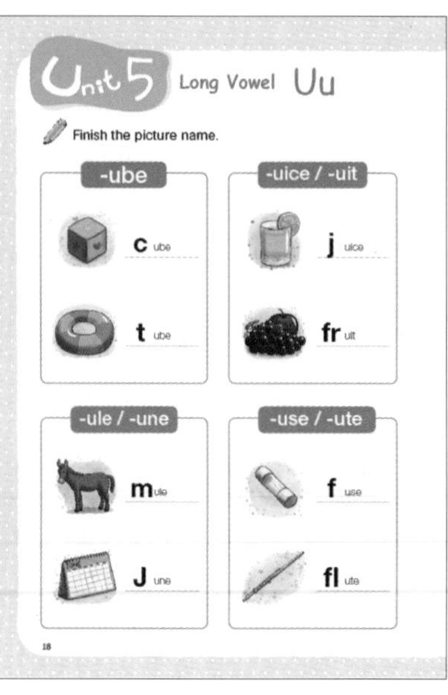

Unit 5 Long Vowel Uu

Finish the picture name.

-ube: c ube, t ube
-uice / -uit: j uice, fr uit
-ule / -une: m ule, J une
-use / -ute: f use, fl ute

18

Choose the correct word and write it.

dune — dune / dule
cube — cabe / cube
suit — suit / sate
tube — tube / tabe
June — June / Jane
fruit — frate / fruit

19

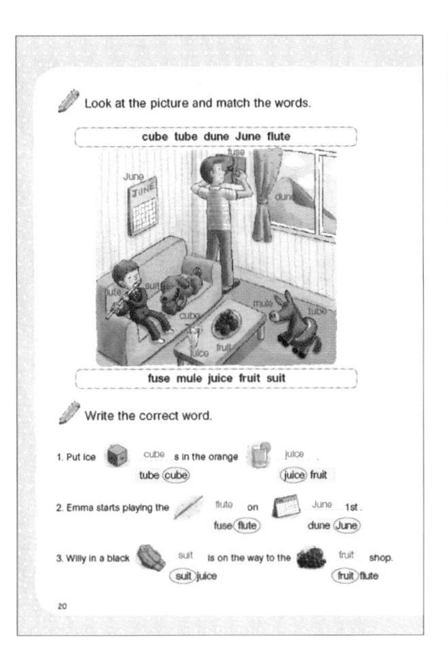
Look at the picture and match the words.
cube tube dune June flute
fuse mule juice fruit suit
Write the correct word.
1. Put ice cube s in the orange juice .
tube cube juice fruit
2. Emma starts playing the flute on June 1st .
fuse flute dune June
3. Willy in a black suit is on the way to the fruit shop.
suit juice fruit flute
20

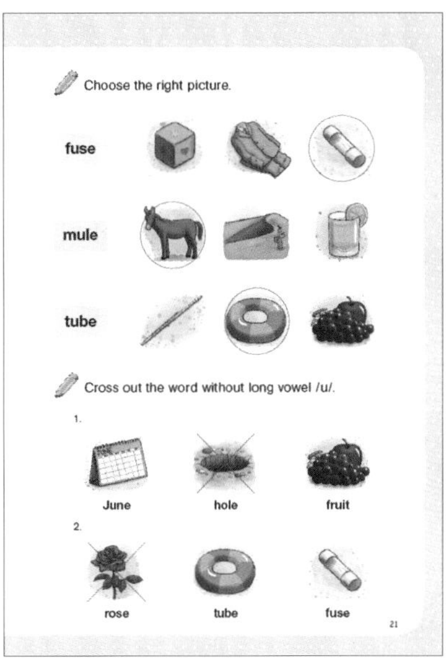
Choose the right picture.
fuse
mule
tube
Cross out the word without long vowel /u/.
1.
June
hole
fruit
2.
rose
tube
fuse
21

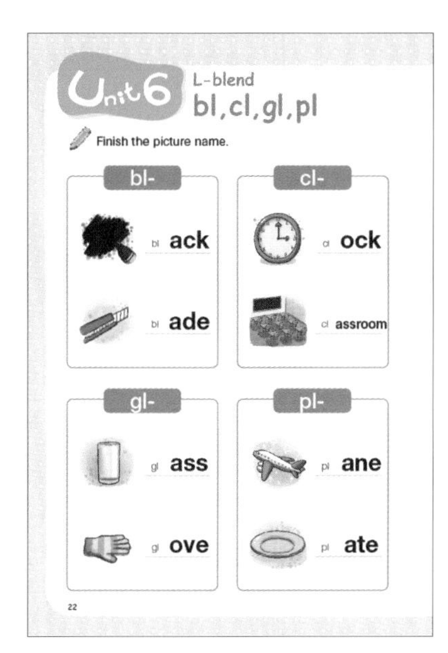
Unit 6
L-blend
bl, cl, gl, pl
Finish the picture name.
bl-
bl ack
bl ade
cl-
cl ock
cl assroom
gl-
gl ass
gl ove
pl-
pl ane
pl ate
22

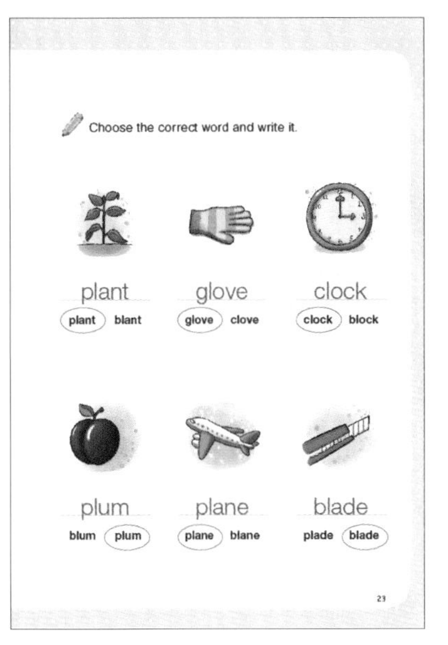
Choose the correct word and write it.
plant
plant blant
glove
glove clove
clock
clock block
plum
blum plum
plane
plane blane
blade
plade blade
23

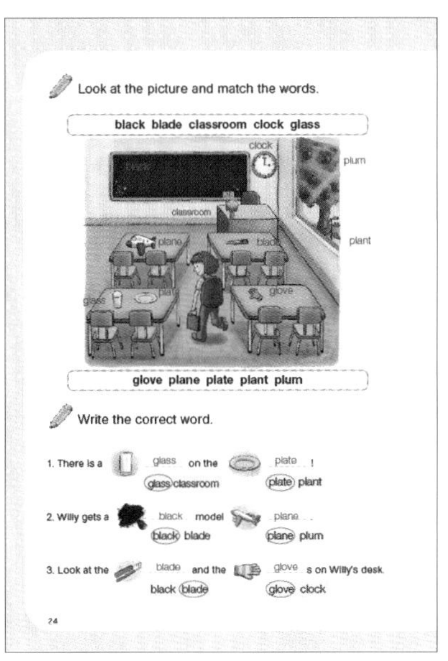
Look at the picture and match the words.
black blade classroom clock glass
glove plane plate plant plum
Write the correct word.
1. There is a glass on the plate !
glass classroom plate plant
2. Willy gets a black model plane .
black blade plane plum
3. Look at the blade and the glove s on Willy's desk.
black blade glove clock
24

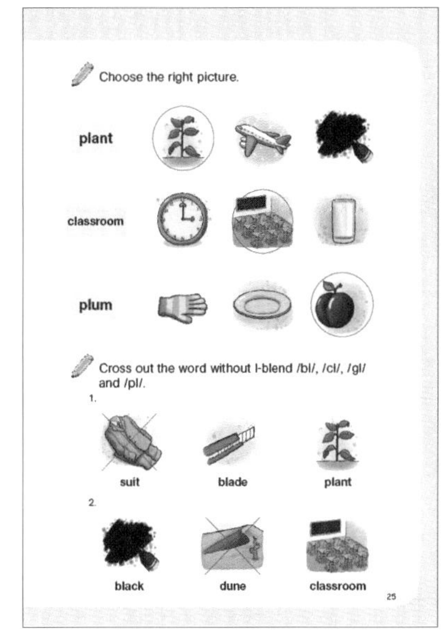
Choose the right picture.
plant
classroom
plum
Cross out the word without l-blend /bl/, /cl/, /gl/ and /pl/.
1.
suit
blade
plant
2.
black
dune
classroom
25

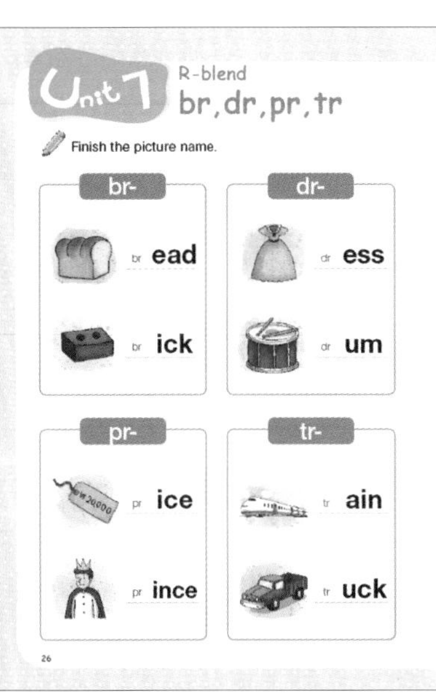
Unit 7
R-blend
br, dr, pr, tr
Finish the picture name.
br-
br ead
br ick
dr-
dr ess
dr um
pr-
pr ice
pr ince
tr-
tr ain
tr uck
26

Choose the correct word and write it.
brush
brush drush
dress
press dress
bride
tride bride
bread
bread dread
truck
bruck truck
price
drice price
27

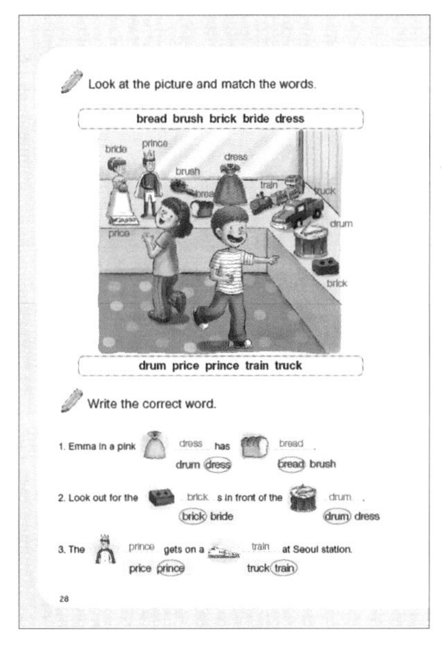
Look at the picture and match the words.
bread brush brick bride dress
drum price prince train truck
Write the correct word.
1. Emma in a pink dress has bread .
drum dress bread brush
2. Look out for the brick s in front of the drum .
brick bride drum dress
3. The prince gets on a train at Seoul station.
price prince truck train
28

Choose the right picture.
dress
truck
brush
Cross out the word without r-blend /br/, /dr/, /pr/ and /tr/.
1.
plum
price
prince
2.
drum
glove
train
29

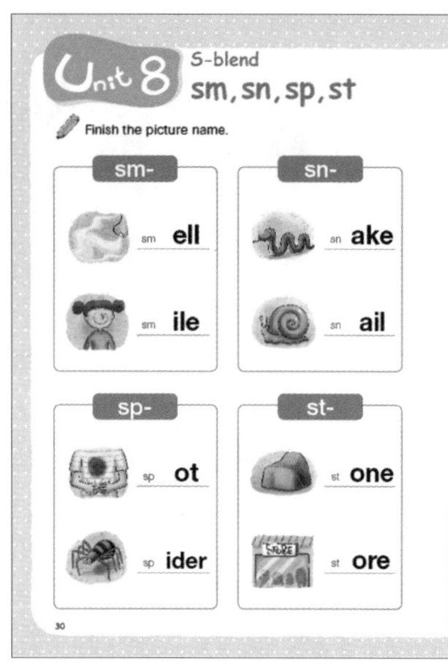
Unit 8
S-blend
sm, sn, sp, st
Finish the picture name.
sm-
sm ell
sm ile
sn-
sn ake
sn ail
sp-
sp ot
sp ider
st-
st one
st ore
30

Choose the correct word and write it.
smile
smile snile
store
spore store
spider
spider stider
stove
spove stove
stop
snop stop
smell
snell smell
31

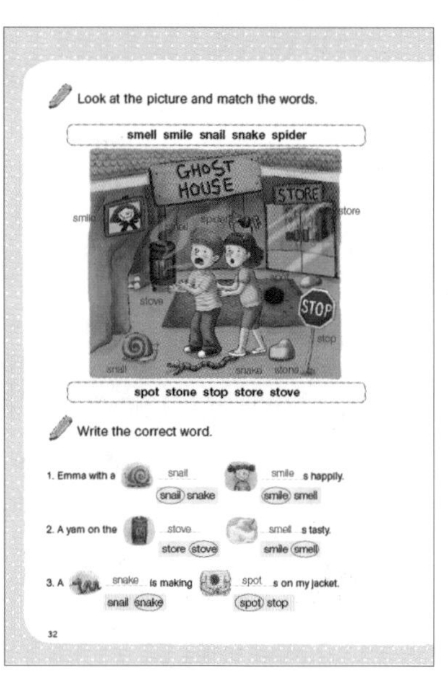
Look at the picture and match the words.
smell smile snail snake spider
GHOST HOUSE
STORE
STOP
spot stone stop store stove
Write the correct word.
1. Emma with a snail smile s happily.
snail snake smile smell
2. A yam on the stove smell s tasty.
store stove smile smell
3. A snake is making spot s on my jacket.
snail snake spot stop
32

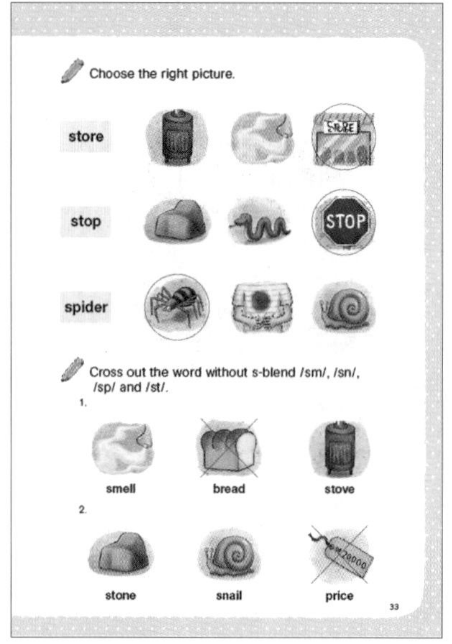
Choose the right picture.
store
stop
spider
Cross out the word without s-blend /sm/, /sn/, /sp/ and /st/.
1.
smell
bread
stove
2.
stone
snail
price
33

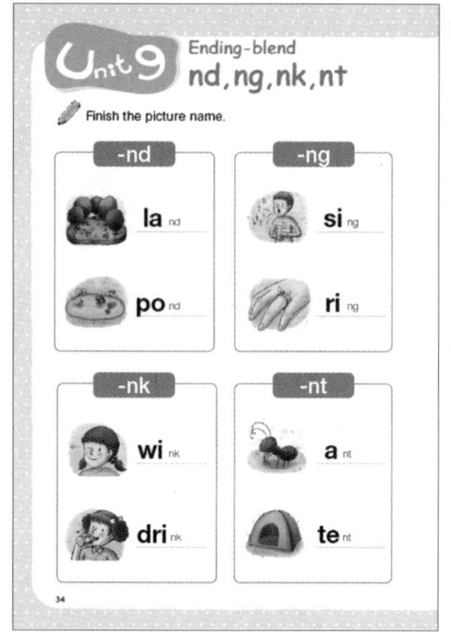
Unit 9
Ending-blend
nd, ng, nk, nt
Finish the picture name.
-nd
la nd
po nd
-ng
si ng
ri ng
-nk
wi nk
dri nk
-nt
a nt
te nt
34

Choose the correct word and write it.
long
lond long
drink
drind drink
ring
ring rink
pond
pond pont
sing
sink sing
wing
wing wind
35

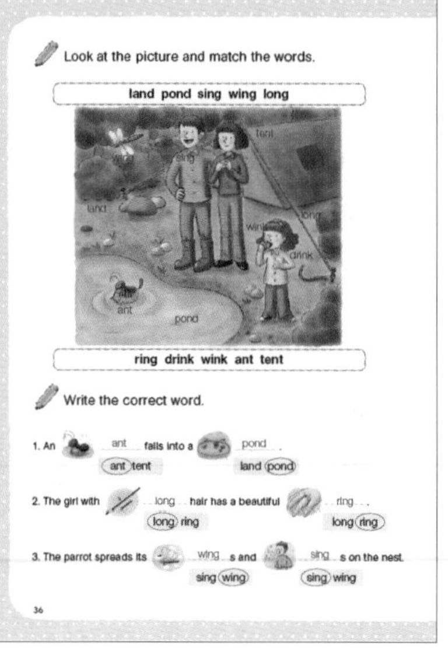
Look at the picture and match the words.
land pond sing wing long
ring drink wink ant tent
Write the correct word.
1. An ant falls into a pond.
ant tent land pond
2. The girl with long hair has a beautiful ring.
long ring long ring
3. The parrot spreads its wing s and sing s on the nest.
sing wing sing wing
36

Choose the right picture.
wink
land
tent
Cross out the word without ending-blend /nd/, /ng/, /nk/ and /nt/.
1.
sing
drink
smile
2.
ant
spot
pond
37

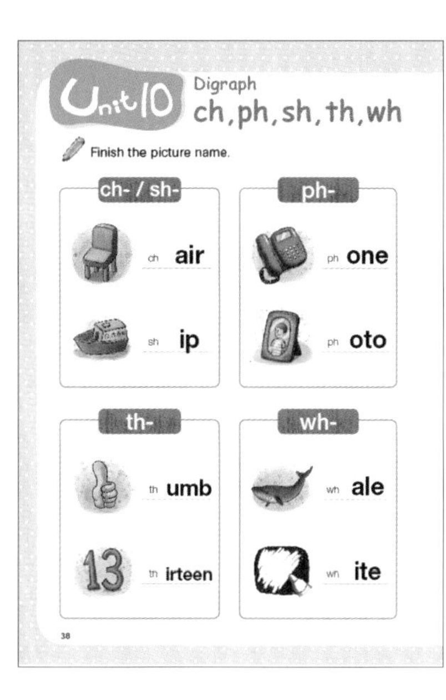
Unit 10 Digraph
ch, ph, sh, th, wh

Finish the picture name.

ch- / sh-
ch air
sh ip

ph-
ph one
ph oto

th-
th umb
th irteen

wh-
wh ale
wh ite

38

Choose the correct word and write it.

cheese — pheese (cheese)
white — (white) chite
shell — chell (shell)
phone — (phone) thone
chair — whair (chair)
photo — choto (photo)

39

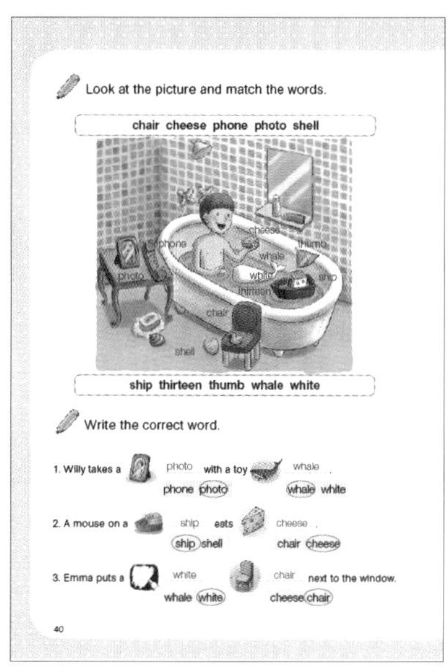
Look at the picture and match the words.

chair cheese phone photo shell

ship thirteen thumb whale white

Write the correct word.

1. Willy takes a photo with a toy whale.
phone (photo) — (whale) white

2. A mouse on a ship eats cheese.
(ship) shell — chair (cheese)

3. Emma puts a white chair next to the window.
whale (white) — cheese (chair)

40

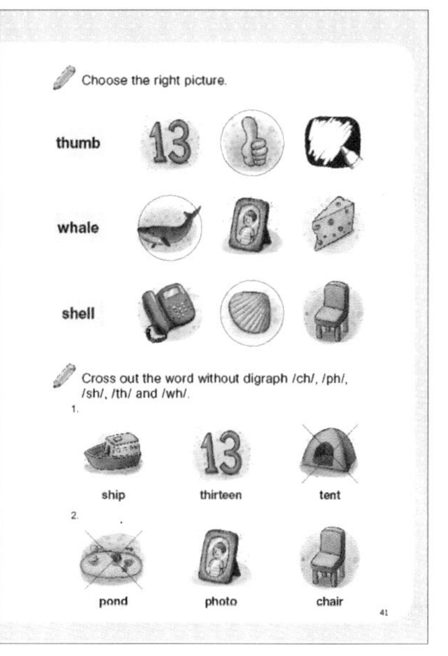
Choose the right picture.

thumb

whale

shell

Cross out the word without digraph /ch/, /ph/, /sh/, /th/ and /wh/.

1. ship thirteen tent
2. pond photo chair

41

Unit 11 Double Letter Vowels
oa, ow

Finish the picture name.

-oa-
b oa t
g oa t
c oa t
s oa p

-ow
sn ow
pill ow
yell ow
wind ow

42

Choose the correct word and write it.

toast — (toast) toust
bowl — (bowl) boast
coat — cout (coat)
snow — (snow) snaw
soap — (soap) soup
pillow — pillaw (pillow)

43

Look at the picture and match the words.

boat coat goat soap toast

bowl pillow snow window yellow

Write the correct word.

1. The house has yellow windows.
pillow (yellow) — snow (window)

2. Willy in a rain coat plays in the snow.
boat (coat) — pillow (snow)

3. Mom cleans a bowl with a dish soap.
(bowl) pillow — (soap) goat

44

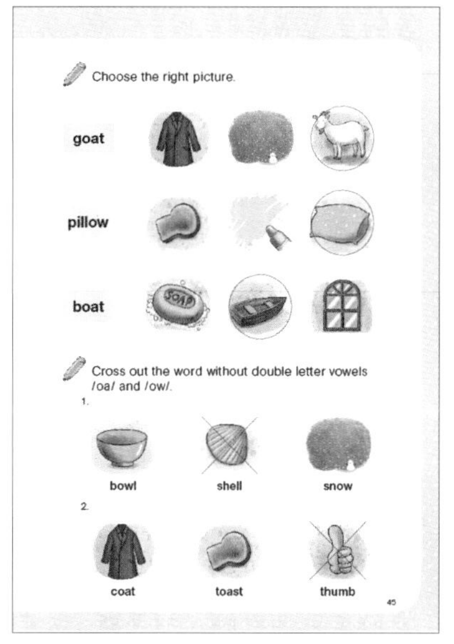
Choose the right picture.

goat

pillow

boat

Cross out the word without double letter vowels /oa/ and /ow/.

1. bowl shell snow
2. coat toast thumb

45

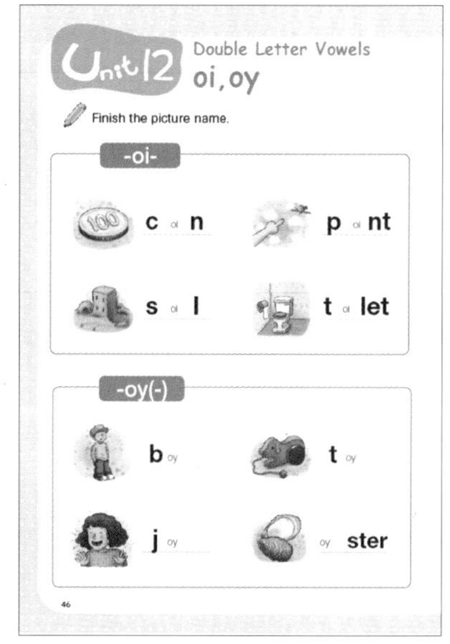
Unit 12 Double Letter Vowels
oi, oy

Finish the picture name.

-oi-
c oi n
p oi nt
s oi l
t oi let

-oy(-)
b oy
t oy
j oy
oy ster

46

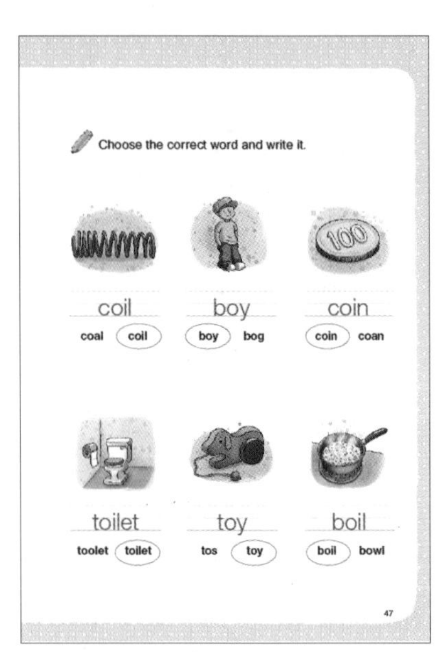
Choose the correct word and write it.

coil — coal / coil
boy — boy / bog
coin — coin / coan
toilet — toolet / toilet
toy — tos / toy
boil — boil / bowl

47

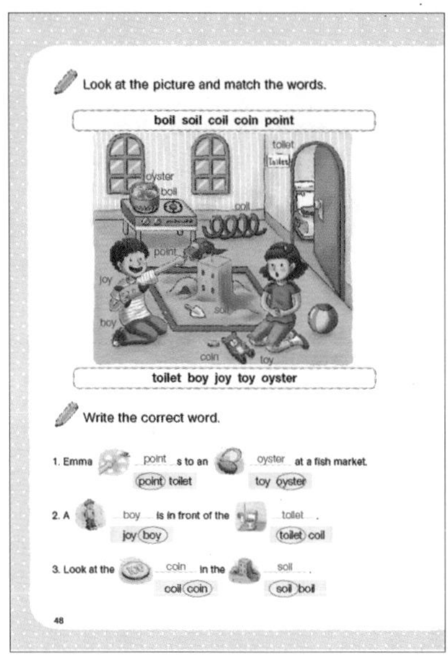
Look at the picture and match the words.

boil soil coil coin point

toilet boy joy toy oyster

Write the correct word.

1. Emma point s to an oyster at a fish market. (point / toilet) (toy / oyster)
2. A boy is in front of the toilet. (joy / boy) (toilet / coil)
3. Look at the coin in the soil. (coil / coin) (soil / boil)

48

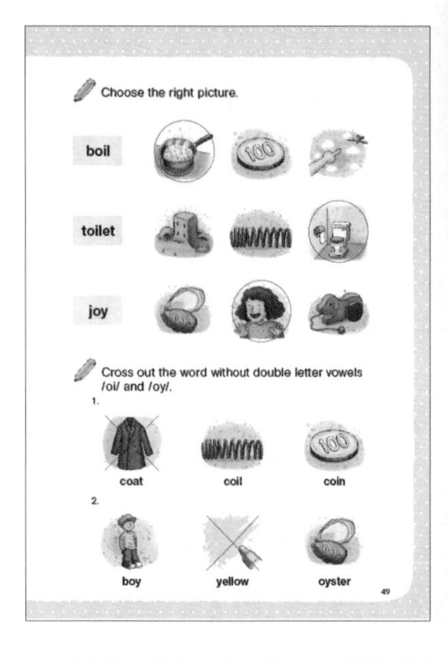
Choose the right picture.

boil

toilet

joy

Cross out the word without double letter vowels /oi/ and /oy/.

1. coat coil coin
2. boy yellow oyster

49

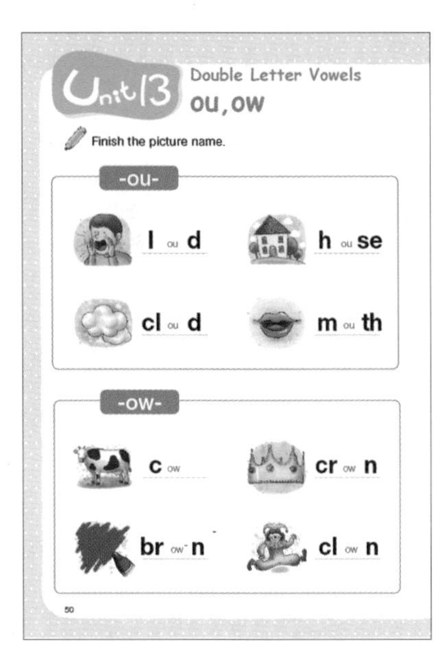
Unit 13 Double Letter Vowels ou, ow

Finish the picture name.

-ou-

l ou d
h ou se
cl ou d
m ou th

-ow-

c ow
cr ow n
br ow n
cl ow n

50

Choose the correct word and write it.

house — house / hose
brown — brown / broun
cloud — cloud / clod
mouth — mouth / month
gown — goun / gown
owl — owl / oil

51

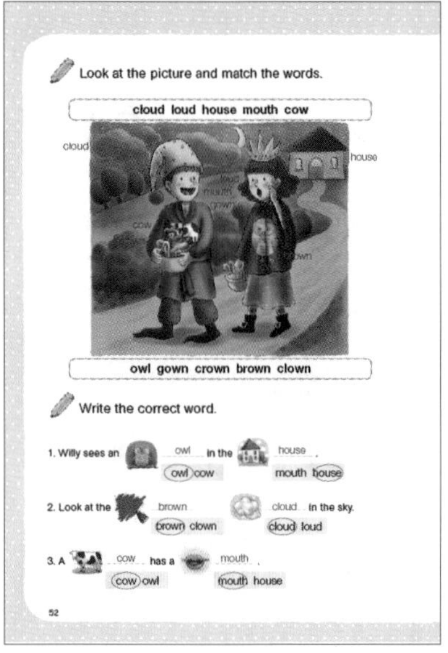
Look at the picture and match the words.

cloud loud house mouth cow

owl gown crown brown clown

Write the correct word.

1. Willy sees an owl in the house. (owl / cow) (mouth / house)
2. Look at the brown cloud in the sky. (brown / clown) (cloud / loud)
3. A cow has a mouth. (cow / owl) (mouth / house)

52

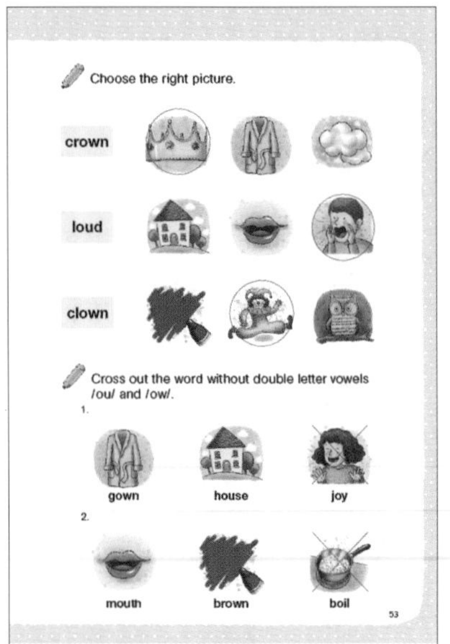
Choose the right picture.

crown

loud

clown

Cross out the word without double letter vowels /ou/ and /ow/.

1. gown house joy
2. mouth brown boil

53

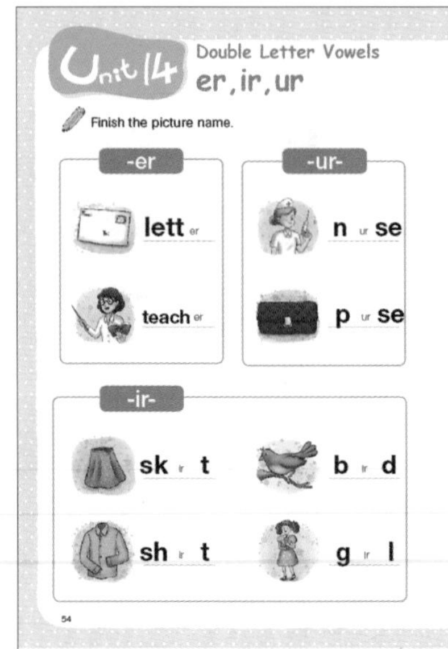
Unit 14 Double Letter Vowels er, ir, ur

Finish the picture name.

-er-

lett er
teach er

-ur-

n ur se
p ur se

-ir-

sk ir t
b ir d
sh ir t
g ir l

54

Choose the correct word and write it.

farmer — farmer / farmur
girl — girl / gerl
nurse — nirse / nurse
singer — singur / singer
purse — perse / purse
bird — berd / bird

55

Look at the picture and match the words.

letter singer farmer teacher bird

girl shirt skirt nurse purse

Write the correct word.

1. My teacher sent me a letter.
nurse teacher / letter singer

2. A farmer feeds bread to the birds.
farmer singer / girl bird

3. The singer likes to wear a skirt.
farmer singer / skirt shirt

56

Choose the right picture.

purse

skirt

singer

Cross out the word without double letter vowels /er/, /ir/ and /ur/.

1.
shirt cow bird

2.
farmer nurse cloud

57

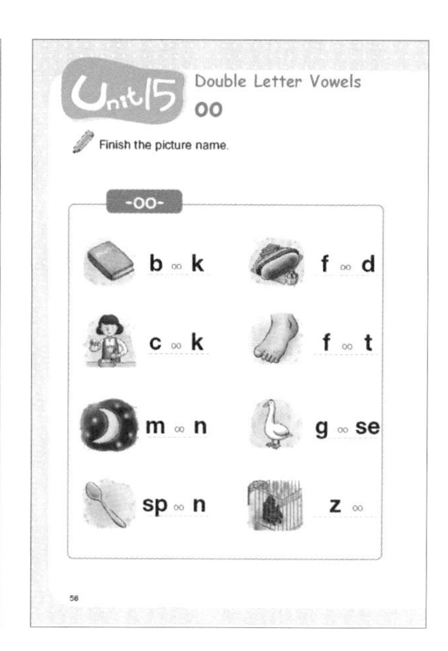

Unit 15 Double Letter Vowels
oo

Finish the picture name.

-oo-

b oo k f oo d
c oo k f oo t
m oo n g oo se
sp oo n z oo

58

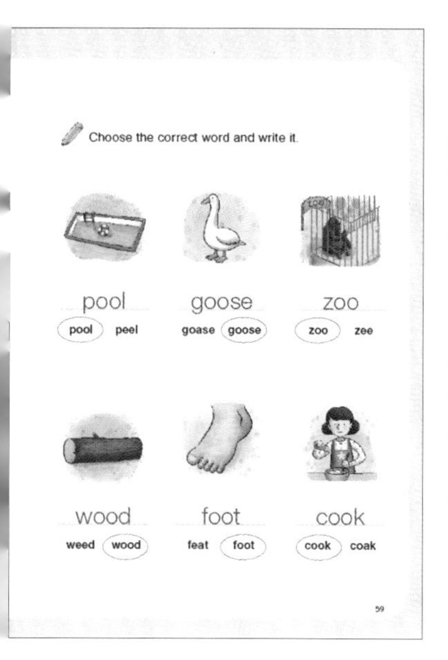

Choose the correct word and write it.

pool	goose	zoo
pool peel	goase goose	zoo zee

wood	foot	cook
weed wood	feat foot	cook coak

59

Look at the picture and match the words.

book cook food foot goose

moon pool spoon wood zoo

Write the correct word.

1. Mom cooks food.
cook book / foot food

2. A goose swims in the pool.
goose moon / spoon pool

3. Willy lost his book in a zoo.
book cook / wood zoo

60

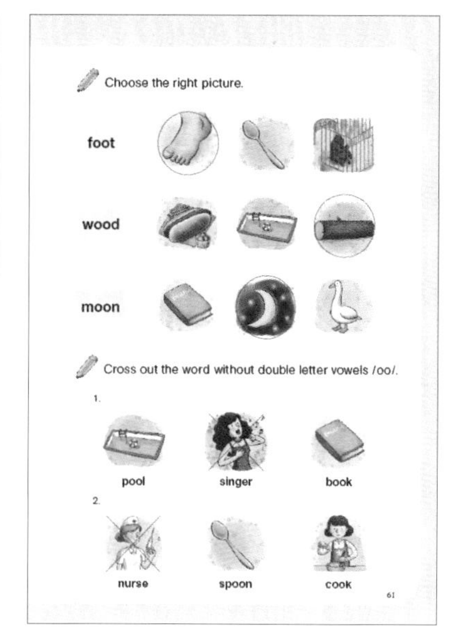

Choose the right picture.

foot

wood

moon

Cross out the word without double letter vowels /oo/.

1.
pool singer book

2.
nurse spoon cook

61

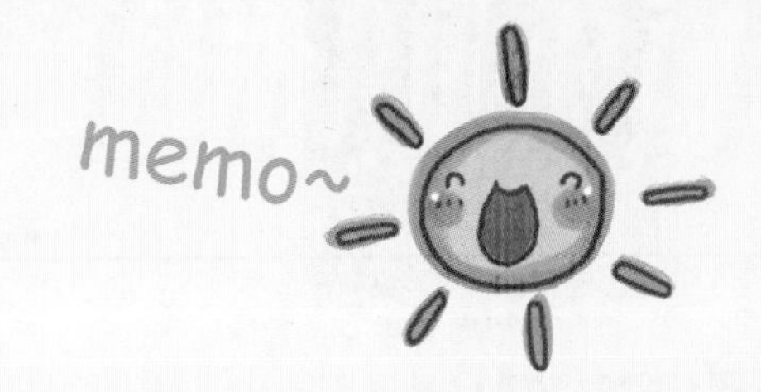
memo~

memo~

Put wings on your phonics!

Wing Wing Phonics 3